Living World War II
ONE FAMILY IN WESTON, CONNECTICUT
Memorable Letters and Experiences

W. Scott Hill

Notes and Recollections
compiled by Louise Hill (Lisa) Paulson

Thistlefield Books

Living World War II
One Family in Weston, Connecticut
Memorable Letters and Experiences
Copyright © 2014 by Lisa Paulson

All rights reserved. No part or images may be utilized or reproduced in any form or by any means (electronic or mechanical, including photocopying or recording) or by any information storage and retrieval systems, without written permission from the author.

All photos, unless otherwise noted, are from the Hill family collection. Portrait of Lisa Paulson on page 98 is used with permission of Leslie Faye.

A note about the typeface: The majority of this book is culled from the letters of Scott Hill, and we wanted to honor the old typewriter he used. The typeface selected, Courier, is a monospaced slab serif typeface designed to resemble the output from a strike-on typewriter. The typeface was designed by Howard "Bud" Kettler in 1955.

First Printing 2014
Printed in the United States of America

ISBN-13: 978-0-9816906-5-0
Library of Congress Control Number: 2014957887

Editor: Carolyn Kott Washburne
Design and Production: Kate Hawley, Kate Hawley by Design
Proofreader: Paula Haubrich

Thistlefield Books
Published by Thistlefield Books
W7122 County Road U Plymouth,
Wisconsin 53073 (920) 528-8488
www.thistlefieldbooks.com

Dedication

With deep appreciation to the town of Weston, remembered as a small, rural outpost with colorful, caring neighbors and a wild, natural beauty that nourished me at a critical and impressionable stage in my teenage life.

Also, to the memory of my remarkable parents, Scott and Betty Hill, who gave unstintingly to the well-being of Weston and to their family.

Acknowledgments

Carolyn Kott Washburne, my wise, sensitive editor who, once again, urged me to unpack and examine another piece of my life experience. She saw how the many episodes fit together and masterfully polished them to create an integrated picture of this unique time.

Susan Pittelman, my former editor and publisher, has been a perceptive cheerleader for the project. She read my notes and outline and urged me to turn them into a book that would authenticate the war years as they unfolded for Americans at home.

Kate Hawley. Once again I'm blessed with the work of my brilliant design/production editor, who has lovingly crafted another handsome volume. She meshes the text and evocative wartime photos for a nostalgic glimpse into the life of my family.

Karl Meyer, former neighbor and classmate at Hurlbutt School, who has led a distinguished life as a foreign correspondent, editorial writer, and prolific author—and who still lives in Weston—graciously offered to look at my manuscript for possible historical corrections and additions that only he might be able to spot.

Doug Hill, my brother, who, though a small boy when we moved to Weston and when the war broke out, is a lifelong history buff and happily joined me in dredging up memories of our family life. He came up with some vivid recollections of his own.

Bel Paulson, my husband, for years heavily involved with organizing archival materials and writing about his own family background and his professional work and ideas, as well as our life together, strongly encouraged me to bring to light this segment of the Hill saga. Over decades, he has spent considerable time in Weston and shares with our two sons my enthusiasm for its special qualities.

Table of Contents

World War II Reminiscences: Weston, Connecticut, 1939-1945
    Introduction 1
    How We Got to Weston 2
    We Settle in and War Breaks out in Europe 3
    Winter 1939 4

W. Scott Hill, excerpts from letters, 1939-1945 5

Recollections of the Weston War Years
    Doug Hill 81
    Louise Hill (now Lisa Paulson) 85

End Notes 95
About the Authors 97

Weston Photographs 1939-1945 39–54

Living World War II: One Family in Weston, Connecticut, 1939-1945

(clockwise) Scott, Betty, Louise, and Doug

WORLD WAR II REMINISCENCES
Weston, Connecticut
1939-1945

Introduction

After the recent publication of my third book—all three of them about our family life and adventures since meeting my husband-to-be, Belden, in Naples, Italy, in 1952—I got around to investigating dusty boxes of earlier family letters and memorabilia. Many of these were from my late parents, Westonites Scott and Betty Hill, reporting to his parents in Reno, Nevada, and hers in Harrisburg, Pennsylvania. Because everyone in our family had a habit of "writing home" at least once a week, this added up to a prodigious volume of saved correspondence.

I was particularly struck by the detailed reporting of quotidian happenings during World War II that my father, in particular, wrote to his parents; he had been writing to them from the time he started out on his own in the early 1920s. This time period was neatly bracketed because it was almost exactly those years (1939-1945) that our family lived in Weston. Scott and Betty were able to move back much later, in 1959, building a house where they spent the rest of their lives, and became deeply involved with many aspects of the town they loved. It was that earlier wartime, though, that was definitive for all four of us. I've long felt compelled to pull out the details that ignite a unique chapter in the history of our country and particularly of our small Connecticut town. In 1939, I was eleven and my brother Douglas was six years younger.

Living World War II: One Family in Weston, Connecticut, 1939-1945

I gather here the archival materials that tell the story, with particulars and vignettes that Doug and I remember, but for the backbone of the chronology, I draw mainly on Scott's letters to his parents. My intent is to give the flavor of life in Weston during wartime—both the thinking about the news as it was happening, and about how everyone coped with the increasing shortages and privations. I also just wanted to convey an idea of what everyday life was like generally for our family almost seventy years ago.

How We Got to Weston

The family had been living in New Jersey since 1928, the year I was born. At that time, Scott worked with the General Electric Company (GE) in New York City, trouble-shooting at regional power stations as an electrical engineer. (Later he became heavily involved in the war effort and recruiting for the company.) He needed to live within commuting distance of the city, by train or ferry. Though moved frequently around the East Coast by GE, both parents always plunged into the life of their town and church wherever they found themselves. However, by the late 1930s, they became increasingly uncomfortable with the narrow-minded WASP culture of their New Jersey town and felt this was an unhealthy climate for their children to grow up in.

They began to research options, hearing favorable reports about the diversity and values around the southern Connecticut shore. In 1938, they made an exploratory trip to the area. Betty dropped into the Westport post office, thinking that here she might glean useful, specific information. Striking up a conversation with a person in line, she asked where the best schools were. The answer was immediate: Go to Weston.

So they were off to check out this small, very rural village just north of Westport with something like 750 inhabitants. A majority seemed to be either long-time natives (mainly farmers), with deep roots in the land, or creative artists—writers, musicians, painters, craftspeople, dancers, entertainers. There weren't many regular New York commuters; the business and media people came later. Weston had no stores, not even a post office. Fairly recently, in 1934, the Horace C. Hurlbutt Jr. Elementary School had been built to replace the seven one-room schoolhouses scattered around. Scott and Betty found an appealing but dilapidated place for rent at the north end of Lyons Plains Road—supposedly built in 1775 and once serving as a stage station. (After some historical research, Ronald Mansbridge later ascertained that our road was actually Lyons *Plain*, but I'm only comfortable with what we called it back then.) The house was located strategically at the juncture of Kellogg Hill Road, Valley Forge Road, and Davis Hill Road. It had the added attraction of including a community swimming hole carved out of the meandering Saugatuck River just over the embankment from the kitchen door. The owner of the house was Ruth Fox, whose Treadwell family homestead stood across the road; Mrs. Fox agreed to rent to us for seventy dollars a month. We were thrilled to move there in September 1939, just in time for the opening of school.

The ceilings of the house were low, possibly under seven feet. My small bedroom in the northeast corner was sheltered by a towering Douglas fir that moaned and sighed in the wind. Eventually that tree came down, along with the gnarled apple tree strategically marking the center spot where the four intersecting roads came together. It was in this room that I began to dream of acquiring a small herd of goats (a dream that eventually came true).

We Settle in and War Breaks out in Europe

The Treadwells entertained us with the local lore: about the hermit who used to live in a cave under Bold Rock, the cliff that rose on the other side of the river, and who raised bees; and about Fred Davis, the bearded "wild man" who had a lonely shack across from the gorge up Valley Forge Road and made a few dollars digging graves behind Emmanuel Episcopal Church.

I began to ride the school bus across town to Hurlbutt School and found myself in a combined classroom of forty-two pupils—fifth and sixth grades. Doug started kindergarten.

In that same month, September 1939, Germany invaded Poland and World War II began. The general sense in America seemed to be that the war was remote from us. People weren't very worried.

Winter 1939

As the cold weather set in, I was more excited about my new figure skates and hiking up Kellogg Hill with my mother to practice our figure 3's and 8's on the Adams pond. At one point that year, the ice on the river broke up, and the flooding waters left slabs of ice in the woods and scarred the trees with sharp shards.

Our fuel was coal, and we managed to keep the temperature downstairs at 70 degrees, but we saved by heating the upper bedrooms only part of the time.

From this point, I'll trace our day-to-day life and events primarily through the regular Sunday letters my father typed to his parents in Reno. I'll begin with his review of the normal morning routine for getting to work in New York, established soon after our arrival:

W. Scott Hill

Winter 1939
Up at 6:15. Shower. Check and stoke the furnace. Hear the news on the Philco [radio]. Breakfast at 7:00 while listening to the "Sunrise Symphony" [a regular early morning NYC radio program]. Check the river level. Out by 7:20 in the "Puddle Jumper" [a 1933 Ford roadster], pulling up my lap robe and waving to the family lined up at three windows, L [Louise/now I'm Lisa] making a funny face. I enjoy glimpses of the river, the hills, the rising sun and bridges as I make the eight-mile run to the Westport railway station. Commuter cars are increasing in Westport, and I find congestion at the station. Landing a parking spot is often difficult. Toward the end of the one-hour train ride to Grand Central Station, men start putting on their hats. We arrive at 8:46, and I collect my briefcase and newspapers, having covered the news and taken a brief nap. At 9:01, I'm stepping into the GE building at 51st St. and Lexington Ave.

February 1940
After a huge snowstorm, had to put on chains to get the Ford out. I've learned to always carry chains, a shovel, and extra gas. L had her friend Barbara out from New Jersey, and for two days they talked

boys, made up skits, skated, skied on the Amersbach Hill, and climbed to the top of Bold Rock. Betty has been collecting 78 rpm classical records with coupons from *The Saturday Evening Post*, but we can't afford a record player yet.

We've joined the Norfield Congregational Church across town, where a discussion group on war and peace has just been started.

March 1940
A sleet storm cut the power lines, and Betty began cooking in our huge, colonial fireplace. It's helpful to have the swinging crane to hold a pot over the flames, and the Dutch oven to keep food warm. We've been hauling water from the river and lighting candles. After a week—still no power and the school closed because of no heat—Betty and the kids drove to Harrisburg [to Betty's parents]. I came home every night, built up the fire to keep the furnace going, and ate with friends who did have electricity. The damage from this storm has actually been worse than during the 1938 hurricane.

We see a lot of our neighbors, Dutee and Leota Hall, and their four enterprising children who are around L's age. There are always interesting projects going on in their house (they rent the parsonage, next to the Episcopal church).

May 1940
Betty is the new president of the WIL (Women's International League for Peace and Freedom). She's giving speeches, was written up in the Bridgeport paper.

Now we're listening to the radio morning and night for war updates and keep up with *The New York Times*—but try to forget the news in between. There's nothing we can do until the next phase is settled, so might as well keep our hair from turning white. I spent a few nights lying awake about it, then gave up, as there was nothing I could do at the moment. L gets very upset at the war news. For several days, she blew off about Hitler and the Germans: "Why don't we DO something?!" The children get a lot of it at school. We receive German shortwave very well at night, but I can't say I feel any better after listening to that. Haven't checked since the Norway business. Now everyone around here seems to be behind the defense preparations; they're very concerned over escalating events in Europe.

June 1940

L graduated from sixth grade and D [Doug] from kindergarten. Now, out of school, they're swimming most days. First, there's an aggressive game of badminton, then they jump into the river. The current is swift because of recent flooding and high water, but L finds it exciting; she jumps off a rock upstream and is swept down to an eddying pool in the shallows.

I've been registering people for voting. Called up Fritz Reiner, the symphony conductor who lives up Davis Hill Road, and we were invited over. We talked for half an hour; he's short and quick. His wife is a very commonsense person, much interested in her garden. She took us all over their yard and invited the children to come swim in their pool.

I've sent donations to the Red Cross for Europe. Betty offered to take two refugee children for a week or two.

We're getting to know Clyde and Dorothy (Dot) Holbrook. He's the very able minister of the Norfield church where we go, recently graduated from Yale Divinity. Also a fine cellist, he has offered to begin teaching L.

Italy has just come into the war as Germany's ally. This week I attended a battleship launch at the Navy Yard. For some time now, I've been working on war projects that I'm not able to discuss—much of it for the Navy.

July 1940

We drove over to see Miss Walsh's goat herd near Cobbs Mill Inn. There are forty goats, mostly Nubians, some Toggenburgs and Saanans. L is crazy to raise goats. I admit they look very attractive, but we'll have to figure out the economics. We're speculating about buying two young ones, getting milk in about a year, cutting hay from our field. Feed costs five cents a day per goat. We spend fifteen dollars or more a month on milk now. A four-month-old kid would cost ten. We already have an old chicken coop to house them.

We found that Fred and Caroline Poole, down the road, have two goats. A Negro butler and maid look after their twin sons (Doug's age), while Caroline tends to the goats and farming. Curious.

Ruth Fox tells us our house was originally an old saltbox, then was added onto during the Depression. On the same lot, there used to be a store and saloon and the Banks Tavern—a real social hub—but these buildings were torn down years ago. Lyons Plains also used to be a toll road. There was a plaster mill nearby; oxen pulled loads to be ground up from Westport on three-wheeled wagons.

Betty is out at numerous meetings: e.g., refugees, Red Cross (with a benefit dance bringing in Lily Pons and Clifton Fadiman to perform). People think food will be an issue and are starting to talk about land for vegetable gardens.

The family has been several times to the New York World's Fair—seeing fine exhibits in the foreign buildings, the GE show (with man-made lightning), General Motors where you ride around a track in a small motorized car to view the exhibits, and, of course, there were the many rides. Betty found the parachute jump frightening, but got up her courage and did it.

August 1940

We bought two goats for a total of twenty dollars. First we got Bonnie; she's seven-eighths Nubian, a yearling that we'll breed in the fall. She was lonely and kept breaking out of her pen, so we bought Bambi, a four-month-old kid. She's half Nubian and half Toggenburg with tan and white spots, very like a fawn. We rebuilt the roof on the goat house and have fixed the stalls, doors, and windows. The goats bleat a lot when L or D leaves. L loves to sit with a goat on each side, their heads in her lap.

Lately I've been noticing many foreign boats interned in the New York harbor.

September 1940

With an idea of building here at some point, we've been looking at local land for sale. It's mostly $1,000 an acre—too high for us.

One reason we had left New Jersey was that it was over-involved with fixed ideas. Now we find a polarized situation here over town politics. There's currently a slate of seven locals, excluding all New Yorkers and newcomers. So we're trying to get nonpartisan representation, including for the school board—a caucus system.

The goats have learned to get out of anything. I put in new posts and reinforced their fence with chicken wire. L says they watch how we open the gate and then copy us easily. They ate up the iris in the garden.

October 1940

So we enter October and there is still some of our known world left. A few months ago we wondered. I suppose our likely source of trouble would be Japan next. If a few people really knew where Russia stands, then the picture would be clearer. Maybe Mr. Stalin wishes he himself knew. Probably he lives from day to day and hopes for the best.

L is ardently for Willkie while D—to be contrary—is rooting for Roosevelt. Betty and I are supporting Willkie.

We bought a 1940 Pontiac with seven thousand miles, turning in the Olds. My Ford is getting erratic.

November 1940

The other day D stood in water in the bathroom bowl to unscrew the overhead light bulb and got a bad shock. He dropped the bulb and fell out headfirst—luckily not killed. He whimpered for two hours, very scared.

We've tried to get out to hike strenuously or to drive around exploring the countryside as often as possible. Skiing and ice-skating are the favorite winter sports for all of us. There's also been a fair amount of sickness in the family lately—colds, strep throats, fevers that linger. But the children seem to get out of bed to go out on the ski hills even if they're skipping school.

Betty and I have gotten involved with a number of groups and are out at meetings a lot. I ran the PTA meeting this week and FPA [neighbor F.P. Adams] referred to it in "The Conning Tower" column he writes [a syndicated column for the *New York Herald Tribune* and the *New York Post*].

I noticed that several theology students were jailed for not registering for the draft. One was the minister of our Presbyterian church in New Jersey, whom we knew.

December 1940

L took her goats through fields and woods along the river on Christmas; it was 60 degrees.

We finally bought a phonograph—our first. We'd already collected eight sets of records, symphonies. Broke a few experimenting. I also got my first figure skates to practice with Betty and L. All my previous experience on ice, as you know, has been with speed or hockey skates, with a major interest in skate-sailing [where a large sail is held aloft by the skater, who is propelled at high speeds over the ice by the wind] on the bigger lakes.

New Year's Eve we invited the Halls and Coopers here. Had a big fire going and danced to Strauss and Victor Herbert.

January 1941
L has started attending Miss Comer's famed dance classes in Westport—a seventh grade ritual. This is ballroom dancing with an emphasis on teaching formality and good manners.

On a more somber note, I've been watching newsreels in a New York theater—spectacular footage of London burning. Also films of the Africa campaign and Albania. I'm glad the U.S. has not yet been pulled in.

We've noticed that Van Wyck Brooks (who wrote *The Flowering of New England*) has started building a house in Weston behind the Coopers; he has a fine view of Long Island Sound.

February 1941
We had ice on the river (unusual), then rain and it melted; the water rose to a foot below the bridge [the wooden "troll bridge" next to our barn over the Saugatuck that rumbles loudly whenever a car drives over—so named by the Mansbridges who later bought our house.] I stayed up late several nights to mark the heights. The falls below us have been roaring. I moved the Ford out of the barn in case the structure were to be undermined (the water washes up under the raised building). The next day there were ten-inch-thick chunks of ice all over the ground.

It's not unusual for us to skate for an hour on the little pond across the river before going to church, then to drive out to the Hemlock Reservoir in the afternoon to skate-sail. I had a figure-skating lesson; now we're all competing to master our figures.

Lately there have been fund-raisers with events that alternate square dancing and "modern." Also auctions and sales for the war effort that the PTA organizes.

March 1941

Betty and I took the train into New York to see *Twelfth Night* with Helen Hayes and Maurice Evans.

A huge snowstorm. I was out on the (Adams) ski hill in the morning with the Lents, but the sleet was so bad we couldn't see. Then we were out again in the afternoon, side-stepping up the hill to pack it because we were the first out.

I've begun taking my skis with me on business trips (as to Schenectady or Pittsfield), going to work one day, then skiing the next. It's a luxury to have tows here and there.

L was confirmed in the Episcopal church up the road. D made faces during the service and imitated the visiting bishop's gestures, to L's mortification and the bishop's annoyance.

Betty put on a pre-dance class dinner this week. The six couples came here at 6:30, chose partners, and the boys served the girls at card tables. She had made corsages for the girls. Miss Comer made sure that each boy from the party danced with L. I noticed that L was much better all week—more sociable and talkative. [I was notoriously recalcitrant and sullen around the family during this stage of my adolescence.]

April 1941

We've been listening to the news of the move on Yugoslavia. Everyone here recognizes that we're as good as in the war, except officially. Many think we will have a force over there in a year or two. Some think there is a very long war ahead. I doubt there will be any such force and wouldn't be surprised to see the whole thing unravel rapidly, perhaps in a year. Last night we discussed the possibility of a few Allied victories in the Balkans giving courage to the conquered to rise up. There is a lot of serious discussion of all of us in the office going back to work Saturday mornings, perhaps all day Saturday, as is done in many factories and in our construction department. I'll be sorry to make the change, but this is not a time when we can consider personal desires. If we do, we will get nowhere.

I suppose there never was a war with so many opinions floating around about it. I don't think much of the Lindbergh isolationist point of view.

May 1941

I bought lumber, and three of us built a big door for the goat house and a milking stand. Bonnie has been bred and kids are expected any time this week.

On the war, I believe our weeks of comparative ease are numbered, but I refuse to get excited about it.

The kids have arrived: two males. They run around the house, sleep in the sun or on the back porch. Now they're playing in the garden. They follow the children around and generally make themselves at home. L and D have a lot of fun feeding them out of cups, though had to teach them first. They're frisky little fellows, not too sure of their feet yet, and often tumble down the steps. [A sad day for all of us was when we couldn't find anyone to buy them for pets and had to summon a Westport butcher to come out. It was really painful to see the beautiful babies we had named hefted for weight in order to agree on a price. Such is often the fate of buck kids.]

June 1941

L's seventh grade teacher has left for the Air Force.

On a company trip to Niagara Falls, I found everything under guard (as everywhere now). In Toronto, practice blackouts have started, and at the city limits, we were stopped by the police and had to get out of our car. At a business dinner there, the speaker was brought in with bagpipes, there was a toast "to the King" and the English anthem, then a toast "to the President of the United States" and the "Star Spangled Banner." The talk was by a Canadian Air Force man in from England. Canadian news is saying the war is practically won; they play down bad news. We saw tanks, machine guns, Bren carriers, and planes displayed in the streets of Toronto.

July 1941

There were thirty in the swimming hole behind our house on Sunday—looked like Coney Island. Most were neighbors we know, but one had invited three carloads out from New York, including a dog that chased our goats.

Betty has been teaching French to L and two of the Halls, Willy and Nancy, along with Latin. L is busy with cello lessons, modern dance classes, is studying sculpture with Mrs. Nyswander, and writing what she calls a "trashy" novel. She helps with the cooking and is always occupied with the goats.

August 1941

Betty hasn't even one pair of silk stockings now; the supply has been cut off.

At the Westport Playhouse, we saw Tyrone Power and Anabella in *Lilliom*.

Dinner at the Leopold Godowskys (Leo and Frankie), served by their butler, with different wines for each course. Leo said there are new improvements coming in movie film as a result of work he is doing. [He was the inventor of Kodachrome, as well as being a superb violinist; Frankie is Frances Gershwin, sister of George]. Leo spoke of Stravinsky staying overnight with them, and also was expecting Sigmond Spaeth and Fritz Reiner.

September 1941

A business trip to Boston was an excuse to take the family to explore the city. We continued north to see Quebec City, then came back to climb Mt. Katahdin, highest peak in Maine. Followed on to the sea at Acadia National Park and down the coast. I noted at the end of the eighteen hundred miles that we got 17.6 mpg at an average cost of 22.2 cents per gallon.

Back home I borrowed an old power mower and truck to cut our hay for the goats. There was a power-driven sickle bar, but otherwise we pushed. While I cut what was mostly clover, Betty and L raked it up.

I notice that you people out in Nevada are continually mourning over the news. Maybe you get more "scare-heads" over the radio than we do, or maybe we've just gotten hardened to it. At least I don't expect very much in the way of cheerful news for a while.

October 1941
Betty is organizing a modern dance class at the school and is writing to Martha Graham for help. She also enlisted the talents of local ballet master, George Volodine, a refugee from the Bolshoi in Russia who had worked with George Balanchine. Mr. Volodine will teach classes at Hurlbutt and promises a Christmas extravaganza where every child will have a part.

At a PTA meeting, FPA told the story of a visitor who came to Reading, inquiring where he could find Mark Twain—as to a shrine. The native said he'd lived there all his life and never heard of a Mr. Twain. The tourist described where he was supposed to live, how he looked, and that he was usually dressed in white. The native replied, "Oh sure, you mean Sam Clemens, looks like a lion."

We had a group of artists over. Phil Lyford was America First. [The America First Committee was an antiwar movement against the U.S. entering the war or giving aid. Created in 1940, its most extreme spokesman was Charles Lindbergh.] The evening promised to be a stormy one, but things quieted down when the topic changed to art. The next day they all came back to paint around our land. I got out my own paints, hoping to get some critique of my amateur efforts.

The news from Russia continues bad. I wonder which will get there first, the Germans or winter. I'd be satisfied if we were to make our policies from week to week 'til we know what's next.

Betty went to see Van Wyck Brooks and finally persuaded him to speak at the school. She found him to be very shy and also very proud of his new house.

November 1941

D reported going out with kids for Halloween. He was excited at how bad they'd been, scaring a cook, ringing bells, throwing rotten apples at a car (the driver got mad and yelled that he'd throw the boys in jail). D just stood there and told him they don't throw little boys in jail, so he couldn't. When other kids came around, he was hanging out of his bedroom window trying to scare them. So he had a thoroughly good time.

We picked up Van Wyck Brooks and his wife to take them to his talk at the school. Found them very pleasant. She's a lively, intelligent person who seems to be on guard all the time to protect her husband and to note how others take him. He is quiet, whimsical, a little plump with a graying mustache. He told the crowd that he was the world's worst speaker and promptly sat down, got out his books, and read to the audience for about an hour in his good Harvard accent. A few were disappointed that he "just read," but most enjoyed the hour.

I must buy at least one new tire and get another retreaded while there is still rubber. We let it go until the fabric showed.

At the office, we've begun making charts for air raid response, figuring how to protect the two thousand or so in our building. There isn't enough space for everyone, but I can't get too excited. Also, our local Weston committees are trying to determine how many bodies to take out of each farmhouse in the woods when/if bombed. [That is, a count of how many lived in each house that would have to be brought out and accounted for.]

Went to a talk at a Fight for Freedom rally.

Betty and I drove to New Jersey for a dinner party with old friends. Most people there are interventionists, as they are now in Weston. We think John L. Lewis was shrewd, bent on getting everything he could for his union. We were glad to see the soft coal strike was called off. We assume anti-strike legislation will go through, as they seem to have carried this business of willful interference farther than necessary.

I walked clear across Harlem on 125th Street to get my train. Saw no special evidence of the crime wave reported there. I did learn a lot about what the young man should be wearing, at least in their neighborhood: jitterbug pants, trousers that look like ski pants at the bottom with big flares at the knees, like long knickers. Jade green was a favorite color. They wear them to dances.

December 7, 1941

I suppose you have your radio on now, unless you're out in the countryside. You know, then, that the war has broken out in your quarter of the world. Have you spotted any Japanese planes yet? I doubt that you will unless they have surprised us more than the *Times* would indicate possible. I suppose we'll have had some bad losses before this is over. Glad they didn't get the Canal in the first surprise; that would have been the first thing they might have tried. Our company will tighten up some more, if that's possible.

December 14, 1941

The radio seems to have found its stride in this war reporting. Until Roosevelt talked, we had all sorts of wild reports and commentators orating all through the house if we let them.

Things have moved fast and with little or no opposition. At the moment, it sounds as favorable as can be expected. Apparently San Francisco had lots of excitement, or at least alarms. Tuesday we were getting rumors thick and fast. In the elevator, I heard the girls talking: Germany declared war on us, enemy planes are an hour away, or a mile away . . . As we returned from lunch, two fire departments near us rolled out and started their sirens. In a few minutes, they blew again—supposed to indicate the all-clear. An hour later it started all over again, though the sky was perfectly clear. We all went on working and disregarded the fuss. However, I did sit down to set up an emergency call system for disasters so that if one occurs, we can reach out to a hundred men, phones or not. The next morning there was another alarm as I came into the office, but no one even listened this time. We do rather half expect a few bombs just for good measure sometime. I can think of a few places I hope they don't hit—the utility services, and so forth.

Generally I'd say that everyone is calm and collected. No one was surprised, though a little disturbed, when two British battleships were lost at the same time—a blow. A doctor told Betty that lots of people had been coming to her in a state of nerves. There was feverish activity for a few days by the air raid wardens in New York to find out what they should be doing, but now they know and have settled back. Our office stays in the corridor on the twentieth floor (ours), and one person stands at the setback roof to put out incendiaries. I've taken to carrying a pocket flashlight. Such are my preparations for participating in the latest war.

Christmas 1941

D has been leaning over my shoulder, pasting in his dollar's worth of defense stamps. We'll get another batch for L. I've signed up to divert twenty dollars a month from my salary for Defense Bonds. I called the Union Jack Club expecting to get a British sailor or two to come out for Christmas, but they were way oversubscribed.

D is happy with his war equipment. We got him a tin hat with some soap coupons and some rubber boots for winter that go over his shoes. Someone sent him a model battleship and an army tractor. So much for Christmas in wartime, the first since 1917. The children are fairly unconcerned about it. We've had no more alarms, but preparations are made and organizations are set for anything.

Betty gave me a barometer, something I've always wanted, a good English one. It should be useful, since the weather broadcasts are curtailed now.

At GE we've had some recent big jobs just handed to us as a result of the war. It looks as though we'll be working Saturday mornings beginning in January, with no pay for extra time.

January 1942

I spent most of the week on defense jobs of one form or another. Some are very interesting, but I'd better wait until after the war to describe; it's bad policy to write about these things—the Japanese seem to know too much already. I hope it has occurred to someone to use these months to get a few planes over to Singapore before summer. Wouldn't bet on it, though.

I had a group of men here to talk over pooling our commuting cars to get more life out of the tires. We hear that 90 percent of all rubber is diverted to the war effort and it will be a while before synthetics are available. However, our joint commuting didn't last long, and I'll try to work it out with another group. We doubled up a few days this past week, but I had to stay in town late, so it's hard to coordinate.

We make it a point never to listen to news on the radio during the day, as it just cuts into office work.

L went out with a boy for the first time this week. He invited her to the movies (*The Man Who Came to Dinner*), and she was quite excited. Spent hours planning how she would dress, complained about her profile, about wearing a hat, about her gloves, about what she would talk about in the movies, etc. I guess most of her fears didn't materialize. He recently escaped from occupied France with his mother, a foreign correspondent.

February 1942

We've been operating on War Time [year-round daylight savings time, decreed by President Roosevelt from 1942 to 1945], so it won't be so hard to get up tomorrow. I'm glad it will be light when I get off the train.

At the PTA meeting, I had rounded up questions, and FPA did a good job in his droll way, peering over the top of his spectacles, putting on an act as though he weren't sure of the answer. A reporter from Bridgeport was there and probably did quite a write-up.

The women had arranged to learn the polka at the school, Mr. Volodine instructing. Betty played, and I think we have a pretty good idea of it now. This is intended for a dance in a couple of weeks. Volodine (a Russian émigré living here) is going to put on a ballet for Koussevitsky in Boston.

After the news today of the fall of Singapore, I listened to Churchill to see if it had shaken him and what he will do next. I wouldn't be surprised to see the hours of labor forcibly changed, and more regulation entering our existence. Unless things look a lot better, I guess if I'm to continue working, we'd better start thinking about moving to within walking distance of a train.

I was in New York and heard the rumor that the *S.S. Normandie* was on fire there. [The French

Living World War II: One Family in Weston, Connecticut, 1939-1945

vessel *S.S. Normandie* had been brought to New York harbor as a safe haven when the war began. It was renamed *Lafayette*, transferred to the U.S. Navy, and designated for conversion to a troop ship. The fire was caused by the carelessness of technicians during the too-rapid conversion work.] Called the office and they said all our men had gotten off safely. We were supervising the overhauling of all our turbo generators, motors, and electrical equipment. Eighteen men in our department had been on the ship seven days a week since January, night and day. This is one of the jobs I didn't mention before for censorship reasons. I watched the ship listing and the smoke. Then it rolled over, and all our work was lost. The office crowd was as depressed a bunch as I've seen.

Saturday I went into the Navy Yard. It remains to be seen whether we get part or all or none of a big job there. Yesterday we had to appear before the high Navy officials from Washington. Had expected a big argument, but they had already been in session for three hours and had agreed to follow GE recommendations without even questioning us. All the manufacturers were on hand for the final appearance. We've lived on this job for months. We got the entire order, about $900,000, so I guess our group did a good job. Had about $300,000 on it previously. They certainly worked hard enough, each making the best contribution he could.

Thursday night I got set for the worst as Betty's First Aid class was to meet here, but the snow that day postponed the meeting—so I had a night of peace.

March 1942

Mrs. Fox indicated she'd sell us two acres on our big field, extending down to the riverbank from the road. If we could get it for $1,000, I'd seriously consider it, and then we'd have property to start a house if and when the war ends. It's not the ideal lot, but since we'd never build a mansion, the lot is not so important.

On March 17, they'll have the draft lottery. I got my number, T 2467. So if you see that number come up first, you'll know the Japanese are practically upon us.

Our group of four commuters who drive together is working well. They're talking of bus lines now. Everyone is buying bicycles. I had a chance to buy a secondhand one for $18 yesterday. Was out teaching D on his little one.

April 1942

Went to the defense meeting at the school. It seemed designed to pep people up; had three sound reels that had some instructive purpose. Then Tuesday I went to Westport with some Weston men. They have a Home Defense group there: drilling, target practice, and the rest, uniforms and all. I spent the evening drilling and trying to find out what it was all about without learning much.

Yesterday in Norwalk I bought a rubber hose and a lot of household necessities that we may not get later. Tried to buy some bicycles, but no luck at all; sales have stopped here.

No, we haven't any blackout curtains. We did put pails of sand in the attic to satisfy the warden in

Living World War II: One Family in Weston, Connecticut, 1939-1945

case he comes by. Somehow I don't look for a bomb down the chimney. We may have to black out to prevent light from the coast outlining ships. There's been trouble along Atlantic City due to that.

I've been preparing statements for the draft boards where we request deferments for necessary men.

Yesterday we began working Saturdays, which included, after all, a 10 percent increase as long as we are working.

I've spent the weekend on spring jobs. Digging up some of the newly plowed land. The tractor plowed and harrowed a plot approximately 50' x 50'. Then D and I put in beets, broccoli, peas, and beans. We expect to have corn and possibly potatoes, if we can get any—they're scarce.

The gas ration hasn't been set yet, but if it isn't too drastic, we could show you a little of the nearby countryside if you were to come East.

We pay $13.50 a ton for hard coal. I bought three tons on the chance we might stay on; if not, we could resell or have it moved. I'm almost afraid to move, as we might get an oil burner, which would be bad. [Bad because oil would be one of the first fuels curtailed.] This way we can collect logs and scrap wood and at least warm up once in a while.

Wednesday the kids were born, a male and a female, cute little rascals. L is well pleased. The whole neighborhood has come around to see them, and people stop to take photos.

May 1942

We've thought about accepting your offer to fly the family West and to spend time at Fallen Leaf

Lake [the family cabin in the Sierra Nevada Mountains in eastern California]. But there are too many drawbacks, including taking the children out of school and L missing her eighth grade graduation. Then we have the garden and the goats, which would be obstacles. Mainly, though, I'm not at all sure that civilians will be able to fly on vacation trips by then. In fact, they shouldn't. Even now there is great difficulty getting reservations around here; people might wait a week, and I can't afford that.

It's too bad you didn't come to us last year when we had free use of the car. That's the chief drawback. We plan almost every mile now.

Monday and Tuesday night Betty and I were registrars on this sugar rationing business. It was quite a social occasion. Everyone had a good time; we saw all our friends and people took it good-naturedly. I had Mrs. James Melton and had to do a little arranging to divide up her allowance so she could get her ration books. We met some of the town characters.

We don't know yet whether oil rationing will extend to the country as a whole. Who knows, it may turn out for the best if they suddenly commandeer all railroad transport.

I got my Selective Service questionnaire and will need to fill it out. We've been asking that our engineering department men be given consideration as necessary in industry, and I assume the same will be done for me.

I was in town Tuesday night on problems of salvage and scrap. Also had a very interesting day at Federal Ship, seeing the various types of boats being built. Censorship forbids discussion of such things, but I saw a lot.

On calling around about starting up a bus line, we found that it will cost eight dollars per month to ride the commuter bus (if it goes through). [The school bus would be used, making an earlier run to the Westport station.] Now I pay twenty-three on the railroad, so it would total over thirty a month to get to New York. Life would be simpler in a place like Reno where I could walk to work like you, Father, and have more time at home. So far, though, we're surviving, and are getting by with our ration of gas.

You mention seeing bombers. D is anxious to learn the types of planes and points out one or two varieties, mostly P-38s. Are your United planes painted brown? Our American Airlines are.

I've found only one letter written by my mother from this period, to her mother in Harrisburg, Pennsylvania. Here are excerpts:

May 1942

(Betty Hill) Scott sweated blood on our 2,500 feet of vegetable garden, now plowed and harrowed. He removed huge boulders and has taken out the matted sod roots. I sifted manure and planted cantaloupe and lettuce. There are many more seeds and potatoes to go.

Those blasted little goat kids are so smart. They get out of everything we put them in and go to suckle their mother, so all our careful cup feeding is wasted, and we'll have a terrible time weaning them. The little doe hasn't had anything for four days except stolen sucks; she spurns the cup now. Bonnie is giving over three quarts a day now, and Louise is selling it to a neighbor whose doctor prescribed it. I think L may sell Bambi and keep the new doe, Cherie. Bambi is too temperamental and nervous.

Douglas is having the loveliest time riding his bike. "Oh, Mother," he said, "I have such grand adventures riding off on my bike to discover wildflowers. I never knew I could have such an exciting time!" He brings in Jack-in-the-pulpits and anemones and rock columbine and bloodroot and violets. He's a very satisfying child, but sloppy.

Louise has so many beaux. Monday afternoon she had one drop in. While he was here, another called for a date and was jealous of the first, and a third came at night. Thank heavens we live in the country! These are all nice boys. The one who came in the evening is a piano virtuoso. She's trying to drop another, and he says he feels like committing suicide. She thinks I am such an old-fashioned mother. Boy, I was never like her. I looked down on boys as dumbbells. She thinks they are so clever and funny. But at least it improves her disposition.

June 1942
[Back to Scott's letters]

I hope Midway turns out to be as conclusive as it now appears. I wonder if help will get to China in time. General gas rationing across the country is due to start July 15.

Friday to the Coopers for dinner. The Godowskys arrived on their new scooter. It's like a motorcycle with a small sidecar, except with very small, rubber-tired wheels. You sit on the engine; the car is only a tin box. However, it works; must have waked up all the neighbors when we broke up after midnight.

We're changing our church hour to 10:30 and holding Sunday school at the same time to conserve tires/driving.

Saturday I saw flocks of Fortresses, etc., over the parade in New York. Then that night Pursuit planes flew circles over us while we were sitting here in the garden before dinner.

As to our vacation, we are staying here because of tires and gas, and also the expense of hotels if we were to go away. It's very pleasant here. We were invited to an estate over near Pleasantville in Westchester, but due to gas, we declined. There is no gas left anywhere around the New York area, and won't be until July 1 quotas can be used. By luck, I got six gallons Saturday after stopping at six stations, all dry. Most of them just closed up and the employees went home. Can't even get air. July first the commuter bus begins. It will start at our corner.

We sealed the deal with Ruth Fox and bought the approximately two-acre field next door for $1,500 cash.

July 1942

Wednesday Clyde and I fixed up the Thorp's tennis court on Valley Forge Road. I had bought some new substitute balls that looked fine but didn't bounce very well. They lasted about two sets and opened at the seams, just flopped around. So we were reduced to one ball from last year, not much of a game. This will finish our tennis unless we find some more. Tried earlier to get up two more for doubles, including Frank Adams, who is reported to be quite a player, but he had a bad ankle.

Thursday I explored the woods and swamps west of our nearby hills. Had a fine time with compass and paper, trying to map it. Went in at the Reiners', and after an hour of following old lumber trails and roads, keeping track of turns, came out into civilization and got located on the map. Then back in and after twenty minutes arrived again on a road and knew where I was. I traveled about eight miles in absolute wilderness (no human habitat in evidence). Put up a few markers for the future.

We have about a hundred feet of beans—all we could possibly eat and many to give away. Got in the hay with all the neighborhood children working, so it went fast. Have about three quarters of a ton of good clover; the barn smells very sweet.

To a gathering at Jack and Adelaide Baker's in Westport to meet Louis Adamic, originally from Slovenia. He's intensely political, supports Tito, which has made him some enemies in this country. He spoke about the idea of a "Two-Way Passage" after the war. [After the war, pushed by socialist intellectual Louis Adamic, the Two-Way Passage was to be a blueprint for peace, spearheaded by America, especially foreign-born Americans.] I chatted with Mrs. Stuart Chase. Last month the Bakers had a reading with Norwegian writer Sigrid Undset.

August 1942

I'm wrapping up half a dozen editorial pages from *The Town Crier* and mailing them to you. I told you about Betty's part in getting Ernie Meyer into this job as editor. Ernie is about fifty and has led a varied life. He was in a conscientious objector camp in the last war, had an amusing time being sent from camp to camp because no one knew what to do with him. Has been down at the bottom, washing dishes in order to eat, and has toured Europe and met famous people. He has no reporters, so has to do most of the paper himself. His son Karl comes down now and then to play badminton with L (is in her class)—a clever youngster.

Looking over these *Town Crier* pages, and seeing Ernie making fun of associating with the great and would-be great, reminds me that he could do an article on our commuter bus with profit. Sometimes everyone is tired, and sometimes there is a lot of humor bantered back and forth when you can be heard above the engine. The seats are hard (maybe the springs have been removed), and they are only half wide enough.

I am apt to be in conversation with Chick Gale, who edits an aviation magazine; Ross McGill, who was an assistant secretary of the Treasury in Washington, now VP of an insurance company; Mrs. Maurice Moore, who goes in now and then, runs a lot of the big-charities like China Relief, and is a sister of Henry Luce of *Time*. FP Adams rides a couple of times a week, and the conversation may run anywhere from books we haven't read to the advantages of joining the local farm bureau for the government literature and advice (how little anyone knows about when to plant strawberry runners). Then there are John Harlan, who is defending the optical companies in a government suit—a lawyer with much success in trials [later he became a Supreme Court justice]; Nordholm, who represents

Swedish Railways in New York; and the regulars, Joe Leopold and Bill Poole, Fanton, Newburg, and so on. From fifteen to twenty ride the bus, with extras up to thirty on Monday mornings and Friday afternoons.

I came home from work one night and found a copperhead coiled on our front steps. It was a joke on me: D had discovered it earlier in the garden, so Betty called Fred Davis, who dispatched it with a crowbar, while neighbors showed up with guns and shovels. Although it had been killed, it certainly looked alive to me.

L has a job taking care of Mrs. Van Wyck Brooks' ancient mother every Saturday afternoon while the nurse is away, at thirty cents an hour. She finds it a bit bizarre; the lady crotchety and demanding.

I have a new raise of $700. Saturdays are additional, plus bonuses, so we get by, but there are no extras or luxuries. We are able to save some for trouble ahead.

GE is engineering the synthetic rubber plants in New York.

Betty has gotten a water glass and is putting down some eggs. [This was liquid sodium silicate used to store fresh eggs for extended periods, sometimes months.] They say they'll be up to $1.20 a dozen by this winter. She buys at fifty-five cents now. A woman nearby sells hers for forty cents.

Betty gave me linen handkerchiefs for my birthday, maybe the last we'll be able to get.

September 1942

L started junior high school in Westport. Likes Latin and public speaking best, and has the most trouble with algebra. Willie Hall was elected room president; L is secretary.

Nelson Sprackling, a noted musician here, wanted to help the war effort, and is now working in a factory sixty-six hours a week on a night shift making machine guns.

I had an interesting day this week at one of the aircraft plants. Spent the day there on some trouble with our equipment for the turrets. Most of the time we were up on the planes as they stood on the apron, completed and about ready to be flown away. I didn't get a flight, but sat in all the positions on the planes, operated a lot of the equipment. Saw the whole production process; about 20 percent of the employees are women. Men work fifty-eight hours a week, extended if they fall behind. Production figures, etc., are confidential, so I won't say more, but I was very encouraged by what I saw. These are all for the Navy.

D asked me, "What would you be if you were in the war?" I said I'd try for officer.

He was startled and said, "What?!"

"Yes," I replied.

He thought a long time, and then, "How many people do you have to kill to be an officer?"

October 1942

Near Nyack, they gave a whole town twelve days to completely evacuate to make space for a new airfield. A secretary in our office had just had a baby and was in the hospital there when the order came for her to get out.

Tuesday we had our first meeting with our new class at work. You remember I told you we're starting sixteen weeks of lectures on elementary engineering, an hour a week, for nontechnical people. They're mostly women, some college grads. We're hoping to get some out of this who can assist on office work if the war takes too many men. I am lecturing them for the first five sessions, at least. There were fifty-five.

At a dinner at the Engineers Club in New York, Army officers were telling of dim-outs and blackouts that will shortly be enforced. It isn't as drastic as it will be later.

We were invited to the Robert Duffuses' for dinner in Westport, driving Webb Waldron and his wife. Webb told of a recent trip to Missouri, studying the effect of war plants on farm labor—probably working up an article. Among the dinner guests were David and Harriet Salfati. David is a Frenchman of Italian descent, fought in the last war, looks impressive, very witty. He's now an ardent Gaullist, hates Laval and Petain; is farming a small place, raising bees and goats and pigs. Apparently he was one of the leading intellectuals of France, left in 1934. Guests spoke of Byron Darnton, a *New York Times* reporter, just killed in the New Guinea war theater. He was part of this crowd a year ago, lived in Weston. Robert Duffus wrote a *Times* editorial about him.

November 1942

I haven't said much about the war in these letters because the columnists and magazines have covered

Living World War II: One Family in Weston, Connecticut, 1939-1945

it all thoroughly. The things I know and can't say can't be said now anyway.

However, the move into North Africa yesterday is in a class by itself. We were very glad to see it finally get underway, though hadn't doubted something would be done in that direction. Coupled with the British success, it likely gave Hitler a large headache for a day or two. I haven't tried to leave the radio on all day today, so don't know what France will do. I suspect this is the parting of the ways, and that the Vichy French adherents and the Gaullists will finally have to declare themselves. I suspect the French navy will be found on the pro-Axis side. Maybe we have plans to deal with it. This is an important week.

We were at the Godowskys for dinner last night. The Salfatis, Coopers, and Ventura Smith (the psychologist) were there. After a good buffet while we were talking in the living room, the phone rang. It was a friend of the Salfatis in New York, calling to say that a second front had been opened in Morocco. Frankie G. was so excited she shouted, the radio was turned on, and left on for most of the evening. So the talk was all about maps, plans, and speculations until well after midnight. David Salfati had been a college history teacher for most of his life—was born in North Africa and has traveled all over the desert country. He got very excited, talking and listening, and stamping his feet. Has no use for the Germans. He could make no guess as to how much resistance there would be.

Someone told a story about the Godowskys. When they first built their place out here, moving out from New York, they were continually bothered by quantities of friends showing up. New Yorkers would say they were "just driving by" (when most people can't find it even with a good map). Finally they had so many plans spoiled that they put up a sign at the end of their driveway: "Fone First Farm." Some of their newspaper friends heard about it and wrote it up, and so did *The New Yorker*. From that day on they have never had anyone drop in unannounced, and haven't yet lost their friends; they all thought it applied to others.

Betty brought William Allan Neilson, former president of Smith College when she was there, to speak at the Westport WIL. Willard Thorp and I came out on an earlier train Saturday in time for the luncheon. Dr. Neilson's subject was what to do with the world after the war. He said we mustn't wait 'til it's over to start reconstruction plans, beginning with North Africa. It will be important to not strip the countries as the Nazis do. We must have proposals for help, now.

It's a little early to judge war moves. Apparently neither the Japanese nor Germans are going to sit back and give up their gains. I hope they get a hearty rebellion. It's looking as though the Russians have had a little relief. No one around here has any optimism about a short war—that is, under two more years. Chatting with Frank Adams yesterday, he said everyone through the Midwest is talking a short war. He couldn't figure where they got that. Certainly not from reading the headlines and looking at maps.

I listened to Churchill give a good speech this afternoon. The Italians must be in an unenviable state of mind about now. Glad to know where the French fleet stands; wish they had been able to escape, but it could have been much worse. Like you, we are pleased at the outcome in the Solomons. [This refers to the decisive naval battle of Guadalcanal in the Solomon Islands over three days, November 12-15, 1942, between Japan and the U.S. It was a strategic victory.]

December 1942
We've had a fairly mild winter so far, fortunately for those burning oil. We keep some rooms shut off to save our coal. But today the house was 55 degrees because of strong winds and zero temperatures. Most people are keeping their houses at 60; at the moment, 60 would feel warm. Betty found that it was 40 on the kitchen floor and apples were freezing. The goats are shivering; they've grown wooly coats that stand out straight.

Betty has been using powdered milk for making ice cream, soups, cocoa, Postum, etc. Tastes good. She found a pound of butter, and I got two tons of coal, so we're set for a while. Butter and meat are very scarce.

Saturday night Betty and I were up skating on the Thorps' little lake. The moon had gone under, and it dropped to about 15 degrees. Earlier I had taken my skis and climbed the Keedick hill near us—was the only one there.

We were invited to the Phillipses' for an outing with the "Duffus Hiking Club" (later dubbed "The Marching and Chowder Club"), but decided against going because of the cancelling of gas for cars and the uncertainty as to when we would get more—and

Our house at the end of Lyons Plain Road

Our house and barn on the Saugatuck River

Wooden bridge over the Saugatuck River at Davis Hill Road with Betty Hill, 1940

Living World War II: One Family in Weston, Connecticut, 1939-1945

(top)
Doug and Louise with Bonnie, 1942

*(center)
Doug, 1943*

*(bottom)
Louise with Bonnie's triplet kids, 1944*

Delivering water and hay to the goat house, 1941

Scott and Doug build the chicken house, 1943

Two new suits (Doug with airplane wings), 1942

Living World War II: One Family in Weston, Connecticut, 1939-1945

(top)
Checkers on the porch, 1944

(right)
Practicing cello, 1941

Marching and Chowder Club: Lt. Dougherty, Bob Lamdon, Lionel Phillips, Robert Duffus, Webb Waldron, James Dougherty, 1943

Marching and Chowder Club after hiking around the reservoir: Betty Hill, Ralph Boyer, Becky Boyer, Leah Louise Duffus, Robert Duffus, Lionel Phillips, Mary Phillips, 1944

Living World War II: One Family in Weston, Connecticut, 1939-1945

Betty and Scott on a field hike, 1943

Doug drives Hank Lent's haying team, 1942

Everyone pitches in to hay our field, 1942

Neighbors come to help burn our field in spring, 1941

Living World War II: One Family in Weston, Connecticut, 1939-1945

The venerable sycamore holds the rope for swimmers in the Saugatuck, 1940

(left) Peter Defoe and Doug catch a sucker in the river, 1941

(above) Doug at our swimming hole, 1942

Doug and Fred Moore on a river raft they built, 1943

Winter flooding raised the river five feet, 1940

Living World War II: One Family in Weston, Connecticut, 1939-1945

Doug, Betty, Louise, and friends during dam construction at the reservoir, 1940

(left) The gorge at Valley Forge (up river from us), 1940

(above) Playing catch in the yard, 1945

Betty with Dot and Clyde Holbrook, our minister at Norfield Church, and Amos, 1940

Sunday School picnic in our yard; front: Louise, two Wold sisters, Dot Holbrook, far right, Chris Cooper, 1942

Living World War II: One Family in Weston, Connecticut, 1939-1945

(top)
Catching the school bus, 1940

(center)
Louise (in plaid dress) in the seventh grade, Horace C. Hurlbutt School, 1940

(bottom)
Eighth grade graduation from Hurlbutt School (Louise third from the left), 1942

(top)
Off to ski in the "Puddle Jumper," 1940

(center)
Family skiing at the top of the Adams' hill, 1943

(bottom)
Family skaters on the river—barn and house in back, 1942

Living World War II: One Family in Weston, Connecticut, 1939-1945

(top)
Scott skate-sailing on the Hemlock Reservoir, 1941

(center)
Doug gathers maple sap for syrup, 1943

(bottom)
Picnic at dusk on the Saugatuck Reservoir, 1944

Our eighteenth century fireplace, 1945

Betty tries out the new bench Scott built, 1942

Living World War II: One Family in Weston, Connecticut, 1939-1945

Christmas carols with the Hall family: Dutee, Leota, Nancy, Jerry, Clarissa, and Willy at our house, 1943

On the couch in front: McAlister Coleman, Dr. Ruth Fox, Leota Hall; rear: Louise, Jerry Hall, Dot Holbrook, Clyde Holbrook, Dutee Hall, Clarissa Hall, Dutee's sister Phoebe, 1941

because of our own shortage. Those farther away all cancelled too, but the nearer ones showed up.

Instead we had a nice walk through closer woods and open fields and over some of those Connecticut stone walls.

January 1943

It looks as though the Germans are definitely weaker, that they must have lost heavily, and therefore the job ahead is that much easier than it might have been. Also, it looks as though the Allies have some sort of strategy based on their abilities, barring accidents and too many ships sinking. It would seem that the place to go after the Germans would be in the air and on the land, as Russia is doing, and in the Pacific by sea and air mainly. I expect Japan would be most vulnerable by sea from the loss of cargo boats. But I won't try to compete with the columnists who get paid for preparing elaborate reasoning. Likely we're all wrong anyway, because our facts are very meager compared to what is required for accurate planning.

During the week, I spent a day at one of the new aluminum plants under construction, a tremendous project and very interesting. We have a great deal of equipment going in just now with our men on the job. Officially I'm not supposed to tell you where it is.

Most of our friends are nearly out of oil coupons and don't know their next move. Some are putting in stoves, but wood is hard to get unless you cut it yourself. I have better than four tons of furnace coal, enough to get through the worst of the cold weather, so we're lucky.

L thinks she wants to be a writer. We outlined what she might study (on the vocational guidance forms). Frank Adams was on the bus yesterday, so I tried to get L asking him questions, but without much luck. He said, "I never wrote a short story, never studied English." So that wasn't any help.

I haven't written much about rationing here. We were getting on all right under the old order, had "A" coupons left over. Now the interpretation they put on the new restrictions will be important. We aren't sure whether Betty can drive to shop once a week or not. Obviously there's no going to another's house for a visit. She went to Norwalk Friday, combining shopping, dentist, and skating for the children. We see almost no cars anymore, except taxis in New York.

As to food, there's generally no beef available in town. Betty has gotten it once or twice lately in Norwalk. On Friday, all she could find was smoked tongue, scraps of pork, and a salmon for the week. This cleaned them out. We've used butter sparingly and filled out with margarine. Canned goods, of course, are about out. Sugar hasn't bothered us, after the canning season, and we don't use coffee. Cocoa is out, Postum short, shortening hard, Cream of Wheat difficult, prunes scarce, soups rare. Ice cream is limited in New York. Hardware shortages get to me once in a while. Shortages of ceiling material may become a problem; Betty called down now to say the ceiling plaster in the bathroom just fell.

No one is really bothered by the situation so far, though some working people have not gotten meat for weeks; couldn't get to the stores at the right times.

Yesterday Robert Duffus and Phillips rode out on the bus, came in, and changed into hiking clothes. It was a fine, snowy, clear afternoon, so we walked into the swamp and woods, over ice, and saw many animal tracks. I left them some miles away and found a new route through the woods. They hiked back to Westport, six miles away. Like the old days when everyone had to get around under their own steam.

With gas rationing, any missing of trains probably means staying in town, so I bought a leather overnight bag.

I mentioned Helen Keller [our famed blind and deaf neighbor living in nearby Easton]. On the bus, I watched her closely. A woman (Mrs. Vincent Sheean) got on who knew her and her companion. Miss Keller would turn toward the speaker and talk in return. I asked the companion whether she understood anything from vibrations. She said no, though could distinguish where sounds are coming from. The companion holds Miss Keller's hand, has a code system for tapping out each letter of a word spoken. How rapidly could she signal? Said when she went "express," eighty-five words a minute, but usually slower. Miss Keller's voice sometimes is fairly normal, but mainly it's quite artificial.

Because of the snow, the commuter bus couldn't make it up Kellogg Hill, so went first to Easton and down. There are eight inches of heavy snow. I had thought of asking Miss Keller in to stay overnight or until a car could come for her, but then they did the circle route. I dug our car out for Betty, put on chains, and then it snowed some more.

During the week, I was on some minesweepers looking at our equipment; some is very ingenious. GE is training girls as draftsmen now; we hired a Smith grad. We've lost a lot of men recently, mostly young and unmarried.

Betty just got a roast of beef, the first in a long time. Also some butter and fresh vegetables.

In December, we drove the Pontiac twenty-four miles, but haven't been able to more than start it since then. I couldn't start it at all yesterday so had to push it downtown with the other car. The trouble proved to be something in the anti-freeze that coated the spark plugs; had to be burnished off. Now it's running.

Because I had to take the car in anyway, we were able to justify going to the Phillipses' for dinner with the walking group. First, tea around the Duffus fireplace. At the Phillipses', we left our coats in the room where Van Wyck Brooks wrote *The Flowering of New England*, apparently always getting up to work at 5:00 a.m. We had a good time and got home at midnight without being arrested (because of the curfew).

February 1943

I used two No. 4 gas coupons yesterday, the first of these. [No. 4 gas coupons allowed four gallons of gas a week for nonessential driving only. You had a sticker on your car to designate.] We always have them left over. It was announced yesterday that shoes are to be rationed, stores closed tomorrow. Betty is going to N.Y. tomorrow and planned to buy some for herself and L. She reported that the A&P has no meat except bologna and chicken and fish. The story is that they cornered the coffee market and the government is punishing them.

Our porch thermometer said 22 below; neighbors reported minus 30.

When I got home from work, L met me outside and said the house nearly blew up. Betty had herded the children out and up the hill, everybody panicked. I went in to find the water in the boiler had gone down due to the safety valve blowing off steam most of the day. At night when Betty noticed water out of sight, she opened the valve and let in water fast. This cracked the boiler, water was dripping into the fire and steam coming out the flues. I called several plumbers, found one who got out some boiler solder and left it in his shop for me. When neither of our cars would start, I got Willard Thorp to come down since he had chains on, and we dragged the Pontiac out with much trouble over the ice, pushing it until we got it running. Drove to Westport for the compound, and by 9:00 it was fixed and the furnace going. I stayed up until 12:00 watching it, and got up several times in the night to check. The house got down to 52.

Friday was the first of district meetings at work. I'm chairman and had ninety-one attending. One of the speakers was Clark Minor, president of International GE. He was just back from a State Department job in South America, and I was able to hear about this at dinner. We had known that the mayor planned an air raid drill at 9:30, so we hustled through the meeting so people could get out to the RR station beforehand.

D is busy—in charge of sugar operations. We drilled four trees yesterday. He's very proud of the job, won't let anyone look at the progress so we'll be surprised by evening when the buckets are full.

Betty has started boiling down. For syrup, maple sap boils down forty-to-one.

March 1943

Today, Sunday, Webb Waldron called and said the Duffuses and others were coming out to hike. So we put on ski clothes and walked along the top of the dam—saw the floodwaters coming over, and then hiked through the woods on old roads and trails. The Meyer Bergers came in later for tea; he was just finishing a review for the *Times*. Afterwards I dropped in at Follett's Nursery. Mr. Follett is an Englishman who has a fine garden; he gave me good suggestions for fruit trees. He can't get any help now.

I doubt if anyone in Washington knows anything of the future, judging by how the draft, manpower, taxes, rationing, and a few such get kicked around and reversed every few days. Fortunately, the Army is training men well, and industry is producing somehow in spite of it. Therefore, the world and the cause go on.

I went out and started to take down part of the old, collapsed chicken house. Betty has it in her head that we'll be eating rats in a few months unless she personally raises twenty to thirty chickens. As one of the neighbors said, I might as well start to build the coop when a woman makes that decision. This morning D and I completed taking down the roof and clearing out; we hope to build a new, small one without buying too much lumber. I'm not sure there will be feed for all those chickens. I expect when this war is over, I'll be so sick of eggs I won't even enjoy cake. Every family around is raising chickens now.

Betty and I walked the four miles down the road to see Ralph Boyer's etchings and drypoints, in which he specializes, and some of his oils. They live in a hundred-year-old house with low ceilings and many cracks. Nice people. Webb Waldron got to talking about an article he's writing on Westport women doing war work at home, a project well underway. He's on his way upstate for more material on the Women's Land Army being developed.

The new chicken house is about completed; has moved slowly because I'm salvaging old lumber. We raised it so rats can't build nests underneath.

Have them in the barn now and began a campaign to eliminate them. L reported that one day she reached into the feed can and encountered a live one.

Saturday night to dinner at the Godowskys'. Our familiar crowd there, along with the Jenks (pianists), and Barnards (violinist with the Baltimore Symphony). Leo had recently played at the Chilean Embassy in Washington. Several played after dinner and were recorded. Had hot dogs, as no other meat available.

April 1943

Friday night I drove sixteen valuable miles, picking up one man, to attend the Regional High School Committee. Mr. Banks has been appointed as a member of the school board of Weston, and I from the town.

Betty and Adelaide Baker went over to the broadcasting studio in Bridgeport this week. They're to have fifteen minutes a week to put on any kind of program they want—about women and postwar and peace, I suppose.

Elmer Zimmerlie, our bus driver, was very shaken one morning this week as he reported there had been a fire up the hill from us. The Cochrans' house burned down in the night; the two girls climbed out an upstairs window, helped down a trellis by Chick Gale from across the road when they yelled. But George didn't make it. Apparently he never woke up and burned. Olivia wasn't home, and when she arrived, they had to hold her when she tried to run in. Betty went up with clothes for the girls and got them ready to go to New York to buy more, as everything was lost. Had the whole town there on the site all night bringing food and coffee; Betty helped wash dishes. The ration board said they could have coupons for anything used for the firemen, etc. Betty took twelve of their laying chickens and dumped them in with ours, so we are suddenly in the chicken business. I went up later and saw the three dead dogs and a mattress, still smoldering.

We had twelve here for a good dinner. Betty had saved half a ham, and it just did. Most of the evening we talked foreign politics. There was considerable questioning as to what policy we're actually following abroad. Looks as though Roosevelt has some plan looking toward a weak France, and he is trying to prevent the French from getting together.

I planted six fruit trees this week: apple, cherry, peach, pear. L sold one goat kid for five dollars. The other is lonesome.

There had been little entertainment in town for a long time, so I organized a PTA program: a square dance with Dutee Hall's band and a caller.

May 1943

In New York, they designated a room for us at the Engineers Club—an uncomfortable daybed, but it saves the day when someone has to stay in due to gas rationing. Only have to pay seventy cents for breakfast. The other morning while I was eating, I noticed that Colonel Lindbergh was at the next table, reading the *Times,* as I was. He's still thin, good-looking, hair receding somewhat. He's a member, stays there when in New York.

I was in town Wednesday night to speak on electronics. I was within five minutes of the end of my talk when the air raid sirens blew. We blacked out the room, as the curtains weren't tight enough and we were on top of a high building. So I had to fill in and talked and answered and asked questions for another hour. A peculiar feeling speaking to men you can't see. At 10:00, the all-clear siren sounded, the lights came on, and we wrapped it up.

Seven of us going to the Coopers' for dinner were picked up by a serviceman on leave, so we escaped the driving ban that way. I get a slight supplement of four gallons per month on the basis of my job and coming home late once in a while.

Wednesday Betty got twelve baby chicks, a day old. Has them in a bureau drawer in the basement at night and out in the sun in daytime, with a screen over them. She puts a light or hot water bottle in at night. They're all chirping and running around and eating all the time.

Last night Betty had to meet with the Defense officials, as she is an umpire for a test tomorrow. So I rode along to the other side of town, and while she was in the meeting, wandered around the neighborhood seeing people I seldom encounter, looking over their gardens. Ours is about equal to others.

I may try to build a dehydrator, with Masonite walls, shelves, two electric bulbs, vents, a thermometer. Costs two cents a pound to operate, takes ten to fifteen hours. Holds thirty pounds at a time. This would save Betty's life on canning.

I got the last lumber available. Everything is frozen here due to labor problems in the forests out West. There's enough for the chicken house and a new side for the goat house.

June 1943

Into New York to see *The Skin of Our Teeth*. Then, as I'd never taken Betty to a nightclub, we decided on the Copacabana. After a good dinner, danced on a postage-stamp floor. Watched the floor show, much above average performers. I could do without the tap dancers and singers, though. [Found out later that Frank Sinatra had sung; they weren't impressed.]

Had the Howard Smiths for dinner, eating two of the Thorps' rabbits. At 10:45, I got a call about an air raid alert, so we said goodbye in a hurry and rushed the guests out to make a run for home down Davis Hill Road. I had to patrol the road as usual. Still on after 12:00, so I quit and came to bed just as the all-clear sounded. A lot of monkey business once we all know what to do.

July 1943

A weekend of picnics. Forty-one (half of them children) at the Waldrons' yesterday. Everyone either walked there or rode bicycles (a mile and a half from us). I carried food, including a hot meatloaf, in a backpack. We ate on their island, looking up at the rapids.

Today a baseball game at the Pooles'. We roasted hotdogs on their grill and made ice cream. As we finished, a lightning storm was coming up so we borrowed bikes and peddled home furiously, making it just before the rain hit.

We ate one of our cockerels—very good—along with our own Swiss chard, broccoli, and tomatoes. There are beans and lettuce every night and, of course, goat milk (for those who like it).

I'm taking my vacation here. My schedule is to work around the place every morning and then read in the afternoon, but I've found there's enough physical work to take up most of the day. The garden is in good shape, the chicken house improved, weeds along the road cleaned up, and a bench built for the bus stop and air raid wardens during their watch. I got tired of standing in the middle of the road in the dark for several hours, although talking to others helps to pass the time. We have drills once a month; no one really knows why.

August 1943

I went back to work a day early, just in case we should have some of the gas restrictions lifted. It would do us good to get in the car and drive a hundred miles and stay overnight somewhere, just to show ourselves what we used to do. But we've managed. L has been driven to her cello lesson in Wilton once a week, and Betty has kept up the WIL every other week and done her shopping. I drive every Saturday (the bus run was discontinued since I was the only passenger), which has its advantages, as it lets me stop at a store or the library, which would be impossible otherwise.

Today we drove a carful of people to Westport to hear Rabbi Wise speak. Seats were at a premium in the Episcopal church. A very fine talk, about the reasons behind the differences between Jews and Christians and what was required. Everyone liked him.

We'd barely finished dinner today when the air raid calls came. So while L and D did the dishes and carried phone messages, I sat out on the new bench in front with another warden and kept everything quiet on the home front. Betty dashed up Valley Forge via bicycle, as she was to be a "casualty" to test the wardens and Red Cross. The raid lasted an hour, and she was hauled home in the station wagon ambulance after due time.

Had the Corwins (Quaker friends) for dinner. They were in our area because George had to go talk with the conscientious objectors in the Danbury penitentiary. [COs went to prison unless volunteering for alternative service.] He's been working on the Japanese business for a long time with the YMCA. Betty killed a chicken in their honor.

Betty picked up our new GE dehydrator in Bridgeport. We got one of the early ones. Next day she did twelve heads of broccoli in it and they came out well, reduced to an incredibly small space. We store the vegetables in wax envelopes or boxes to keep them airtight.

To dinner at the Godowskys'. They are doing their own work, their three servants having left.

In New York, we see landing barges of various types in the river. Have I reported on the raising of the *Normandie*? We look at it every day from our luncheon club windows. Hard to see the change day-by-day, but very apparent if a few days have elapsed.

D has been sick most of the week, a slight cold, low fever, which hangs on. We watch for signs of infantile paralysis. Only one case here, ten miles away. Hard for him to see the children flock here to swim every day and he has to sit under the trees.

I stayed in town Monday night to get some work done on Selective Service. Am trying to figure out who has to go next, and the fair order. We have hundreds to look out for.

The trip Betty and I took to Long Island was our only excursion this vacation. Had a very pleasant three days on Montauk Point. Would have been more interesting if we had driven, but took the train from here to N.Y. and then the L.I. Railroad for 117 miles to the end of the line. Were met by a car that drove us to Gurney's Inn. Fred Allen, the radio comedian, was staying there. He and his wife were very quiet, hardly said a word. They sat near us at all meals.

September 1943

L is in Atlantic City visiting Aunt Bess. She was to return Saturday, but wrote that she wanted to stay on. Her real reason was to go to a USO dance. [Even though I was only fifteen, I was able to sneak in illegally with my older cousin. It was a real eye opener to find myself dancing with soldiers who were recently back from the front, some clearly traumatized/dazed and clinging to us volunteer hostesses.]

All the office called when Italy surrendered, so we knew it immediately. New York was apparently quite excited, while Connecticut was not. It seems to have been slightly premature if anyone thought we would walk right up to the Brenner. [When Italy surrendered, U.S. troops chased the retreating German armies north up the Italian peninsula from Rome for three months of mountain fighting; they took major cities, ending at the Brenner Pass bordering Austria.] I can imagine many in Germany are more anxious than they admit right now.

Our big radio has been out of commission for a long while, but today I managed to get it fixed with help from a man in the office. It was bad to be without a decent radio for several weeks. Probably in no time in the last twenty years, except in the days when this war was starting, has so much been happening in so short a space. We thought for a while the landing at Salerno was in real trouble, but it looks as though they are on their way. I don't see any prospect for a quick defeat of Germany from a military standpoint. On the other hand, I get a certain number of fairly reliable reports indicating that the internal situation is much worse than we realize, and Hitler hasn't any more promises to keep them going, since even his armies are being pushed back. As long as they thought they saw his next horizon, they were willing to work toward it.

October 1943

Friday night we went to a Boy Scout rally at the school. The bus ran to pick up people who otherwise couldn't get there. We went mainly to hear Fred Painton. He lives near here, is a correspondent and radio man who just got back from North Africa. Recently he had articles in *The Saturday Evening Post* and *Reader's Digest* that you might have seen. His story of coordination for the invasion of Sicily and of some of the fighting was firsthand, very good.

Wednesday I went to one of the Fighter commands, worked on the P-47s, then went to the factory where they make them. Much like a Grummann plant, but an interesting plane. Saw thousands at work in the modern factory.

Had a busy week with trips to the aluminum company and Edison several times, and appeared before Selective Service headquarters on our replacement schedule. We made out all right on that—at least they left us most of our men doing necessary work. They took clerical, accounting, and publicity people, as we'd expected. Told us that NYC has already furnished 850,000 to the armed forces, 10 percent of the total, which is higher than most, since there are so few actual war plants here.

November 1943

Friday I got home to great wailing. It seems the Thorps gave Betty some red points [ration coupons for meats, butter, fat, oil, and cheese], and knowing she'd have a houseful, she bought a fine, six-pound roast for four dollars and seventy-two points. Put it on the back porch to cool for an hour, heard a commotion, and rushed out in the dark to hear a dog making off with the whole thing. Never could find it. So we're without meat for a week.

Went to a luncheon at the Engineers Club to hear someone who had worked on raising the *Normandie*. Learned that they pumped on the ebb tides, then let the incoming tide do the lifting. I was out of town the day it was moved so didn't see it go.

We drove the Thorps to church today, as they were out of gas. Had nine in the car.

January 1944

So begins another year. Many would like to know what it holds for them or their relatives in the midst of the war. We hope it sees the end of Germany at least; I think there is a strong possibility. The Japanese may be surprised before the year is over.

The first concern around here is now coal. We haven't been able to get any all week, and we'll run out by Wednesday. We found one company that had coal, but like all of them, they had insufficient delivery facilities. There is a bad truck shortage and help shortage. We've brought up enough coal in gunnysacks in the back of the car to last until tomorrow. I've arranged with Steve Gjuresko to meet me with his truck to pick up several tons, if all goes well. If not, I don't know what the next move will be, but we'll work it out. Between John L. and the Administration, they seem to have balled things up pretty well. [John L. Lewis was president of the United Mine Workers and founder of the CIO (Congress of Industrial Organizations) that shaped the labor movement. Lewis led bitter strikes to protect miners. He became frustrated with Roosevelt's war policies and endorsed the Republican candidate for president—making many enemies as well as fervent supporters.]

Betty called me Monday to say the new coal company was outside unloading three tons of nut coal. Then Friday, while we were away, the other company we'd been hounding for weeks delivered two tons. So we're in good shape. The nut seems to keep a better fire than the stove coal, so this was a break to find that out. [Nut coal and stove coal (also called pea coal) are both clean-burning anthracite coals. Nut coal is between the size of a golf ball and tennis ball. Pea coal is the size of a quarter and burns more slowly because of smaller air pockets.]

While L had her cello lesson in N.Y., Betty and D shopped for clothes. They paid nine dollars for a pair of shoes for D that the man said wouldn't last two months. The trouble is that the government isn't letting them make children's things, for what reason no one seems to know. They couldn't find him a coat for a reasonable price. In the afternoon, I got L and D balcony tickets to see *Arsenic and Old Lace*, which they thoroughly enjoyed. Betty and I went to *The Voice of the Turtle*—sold out, so we got standing room; a sophisticated wartime story, pleasant entertainment.

To a farewell party at the Phillips' for the Duffuses who go to Arizona for several months. Most of the evening was spent on a drawing game, especially interesting because there were seven artists in the group and some excellent sketches. There was a board where each drew a picture to represent the title of a book. Robert Duffus drew a very tall and narrow letter A. (In no sense A broad). Ralph Boyer guessed it right away, walked up and made two short lines for the author. [*Innocents Abroad* by Mark Twain]

March 1944

Friday I went to the Navy Yard. It began to rain as I arrived, and we slopped around the boats and docks, doing what we wanted to do. Some interesting things to see. Incidentally, they aren't called "boats," boats being something that can be carried on deck. Nor ships, because in the Navy, a ship is a three-masted sailing vessel, and they have none. So they are "vessels." I was on one of the aircraft carriers.

April 1944

This week at the office has been spent entirely on Selective Service, since we're preparing all the replacement schedules for four states, as they affect our district. I've been drafted into the job of handling the 350 engineers, not an attractive job, but I feel it's important to do it right. We don't know what the end result will be, because we hear different reports from Washington or elsewhere every few days, hot and cold, until I don't actually believe anything anymore. I do know that if they take as many as they talk about in their pessimistic moods, industry and production will get a serious setback. My personal feeling is that in a technical war depending on production, it would be foolish to curtail your supplies—something like burning all your forests to get warm some unusually cold winter.

    D and L both have measles; fevers of 104. Their eyes hurt.

    Bonnie, L's goat, had triplet kids—white ones—which is rare. They've been much admired.

Thursday I was in one of the shipyards where they are building destroyer escorts and landing craft. Spent the morning in the ships. They have things well organized, crews that handle the same parts or duties on each one. Large sections are built up and welded on land, often upside down. I would guess that a quarter of all workers are women. They go around with welding torches or cans of paint and you bump into them in all corners of the ship, painting away. I was climbing down a companionway and ladder into the engine room, and one who was painting right over my head told me it was an awful temptation to spill the can on me. I took a trip on one of the new escorts. They sail them over to the Navy Yard for delivery, so I rode over. They're still handled by civilians until they're turned over. There were a few Navy men on board, and three Waves went over too. I can't tell you anything of the armament.

June 1944

To a war bond meeting here in Weston. I'm soliciting as usual, and also heading up our department at work.

Tonight we're drawing on our gas supply to drive to Bridgeport with neighbors to see the Russian Ballet.

L leaves the 22nd for southern Ohio for two months in a Quaker work camp in Barnesville. She'll be helping on a large fruit orchard and living in the dormitory of a private Quaker high school.

Friday Betty and L were driving to Norwalk to the doctor when they heard people shouting. They saw nothing, but were stopped and told to hurry and get the police because a plane had just crashed. They did and the police arrived. Turned out to be a girl test pilot; the plane was on fire and she parachuted, no one hurt. A new Grummann craft.

Not much information here about the new secret weapon on the Channel. The word on the B-29s getting to Japan is welcome. Our company furnished all the armament and controls on that. We had a contingent of our men go to the factory areas and help get this first group through and out. We knew they had arrived in the Far East some time ago and were waiting for the strike. I'm still not permitted to talk much, judging by the rather meager news releases.

At a party at the Duffuses', David Salfati spoke of the serious French situation. I said probably it is due to President Roosevelt, but he said no, it's the fact that de Gaulle and Eisenhower didn't get on at all.

[Interesting that he makes no mention of the critical June 6 landing in Normandy!]

July 1944

At a dinner at the Coopers', we were all listening to the Democratic Convention on the radio. James Wolf was there; I couldn't figure him out for a while. He did all the talking, was very enthusiastic about Henry Wallace. When Clif [Cooper] put on some of his records of a Toscanini rehearsal, Jimmy sang and imitated parts of the orchestra, then "led" the orchestra. I found he had been a Metropolitan Opera bass for twenty years, now was working at Bullard machine works for the duration, by choice. Then we got him talking about Europe. He was born in Riga, was in Germany in 1914. When the war started, he grabbed things and started for the border. On a bridge, they discovered a bomb behind him, caught him, and were to shoot him the next morning. He escaped, walked for three weeks without food, then went up to some police to give himself up. They told him he was in Switzerland. He nearly starved but was with a group of young men, and actually had a lot of fun. They pooled their last coins to buy stew. The violinist in the group fiddled while cooking—played so well it all burned. Then they organized a troupe and played in restaurants, passing the hat. Finally got enough to eat. He's still full of energy.

Friday we had a crowd of fourteen here for a buffet dinner. The Salfatis brought a French sailor, injured in a plane accident and recovering. Also here: the Duffuses, Waldrons, Ross Magills, Mrs. Maurice Moore (sister of Henry Luce, publisher of *Time*), Terry Helburn (N.Y. Theater Guild), and her guest, playwright Harry Richmond. About half were year-round people, the rest here for the summer and living nearby; Betty thought they should at least know each other. They stayed until midnight, so I guess were enjoying themselves. The talk ran to newspapers, reporting, plays, war, politics.

August 1944

D and I have been shooting rats (that were getting into the feed in the barn). Have killed and buried three so far. They are wary and seem to have left.

Poison was not effective. I'm certainly glad for the gun. I bought a box of ammo by signing a WPB (War Production Board) statement that I was a farmer protecting my crops, which is true. Doubt if I'll go to jail over thirty-four cents worth of powder.

Not much of interest happening this week, so this leaves plenty of time to speculate on the progress of the war. I hope the moves in France are as decisive as they now seem; we realize we aren't getting very complete reports. I expect we'll find that repeated in other places: smash the German crust and you don't find much behind it. Perhaps the real break will come in the next month or so. As Leo Godowsky says, he turns on the radio every morning thinking maybe the great news has happened.

October 1944

Bonnie was attacked by the Leopolds' three police dogs. The goats couldn't escape, as they were tethered in the field. Betty and the children rushed out immediately, as did the neighbors; another minute and they would have killed her. They covered her with coats and waited for the vet to come. Her neck was deeply chewed and all the skin stripped off one front leg. A back leg was deeply bitten, paralyzed because a nerve destroyed. L put on salves and left her in the sun; then they moved her to the barn in a blanket litter. She wouldn't eat or drink, was very patient and pathetic. L is with her day and night, changing sulfa-soaked compresses [remember, no antibiotics yet]. If the paralysis isn't gone by tomorrow, it was decided that she would be put down.

[This was horribly traumatic for me as well as both goats. Bonnie did slowly recover, but she was afraid to go out after this and always dragged her leg. She never grew back the fur on her front leg.]

November 1944

I took the train to Schenectady for a Navy job, traveling with a Naval lieutenant. Saw many of the interesting and confidential projects in the lab stage. Also much of the B-29 equipment, especially the fire-control system. No 29s have been lost so far to enemy plane action.

GE got the largest single order ever a month ago for B-29 equipment: 300 million. That used to be a top year's business for the entire company.

December 1944

Stayed in town overnight for a meeting on radar. Beforehand I spent two hours at the science exhibit at Radio City put on by the Naval Aeronautics group I've been working with. Met the head and he arranged for me to "operate" the Norden bomb site over a projected picture target. I manned the machine gun turret in practice and piloted a plane to control guns on an image target practice, shooting at a plane diving on my plane; also took shots of stars in a celestial navigation trainer, like a planetarium. All these are synthetic trainers, with scoring devices. I started out with very low scores but by the end was getting 50 percent hits.

Bonnie was sold to a good home for five dollars. With no goats now, L is relieved not to have chores twice a day anymore.

January 1945

A bombshell: we suddenly found that on April 1 we are being moved to Buffalo. The entire company is being reorganized, generally for the better. There's been too much overlapping of responsibility, too loose an organization. I'll be the local engineer in Buffalo, but will continue as Assistant District Engineer—so two jobs. It will be a smaller office. The advantage is that I'll get experience running the crew, meeting all situations, taking full responsibility for the engineering of the company in that area. The job will throw me in with the labor leaders.

Fortunately, we haven't built our house. We'll hate to leave Connecticut, the best place we've ever lived. Will be very hard to go back to city life. Hard on D with his great interest in the outdoors, hard for both D and L to change schools midterm. There's a terrific housing shortage in Buffalo, so that will be a challenge.

Betty and I took the train up to look around; found no houses to rent in neighboring Buffalo suburbs. We liked East Aurora best, but found nothing.

■

After a couple more forays, my parents did find a house to rent in East Aurora: small, in bad shape, and with no garage—for forty dollars a month. Close to good schools, though. They arranged with a GE man moving to New York to swap houses. All four of us were heartbroken to leave Weston. We'd put down the kind of deep roots we'd never felt anywhere else. It was this intense experience of immersion in what we saw as an ideal, beautiful community that would bring Scott and Betty back to build and settle there again in 1959—on the land they'd bought next to our wartime home.

In May, we moved to East Aurora, staying one year before GE sent Scott to Baltimore. There would be three more moves after that: to Pittsfield and then to Schenectady—the town where my parents had met in 1924—and finally back to New York.

I found it curious that Scott made no mention of the May 7 victory in Europe, nor the September 2 Japanese surrender after the atom bomb attacks. It's quite possible, though, that these were such huge milestones that there was no need to allude to them in family letters.

Living World War II: One Family in Weston, Connecticut, 1939-1945

Recollections
of the Weston War Years
Doug Hill

(Remember that Doug was only five when we moved there, so his memories are sketchier than mine)

Gas Rationing
- A trip to Compo Beach in Westport, on Long Island Sound, was a big deal. I remember Mom used precious gas coupons to drive the 1941 Pontiac with six of my buds, two on each running board, two in the car, and a lot of whooping and hollering as we roared down Lyons Plains Road. We got extra coupons because Mom was taking graduate courses in Danbury.

Patriots
- A short time after Pearl Harbor, Dad and Joe Leopold, unbeknownst to their wives, went to Westport to volunteer for the military. They were turned away because they were too old (mid-thirties).
- Near the ski hill on FPA's land, I witnessed the maneuvers of Connecticut National Guardsmen, rifles bristling in the noonday sun, scurrying from bush to bush, a whistle blown to signal the end of an exercise.
- Kept a scrapbook from D-Day to the Battle of the Bulge, affixing *New York Times* photos with gooey paste (for my Cub Scout merit badge).
- Dad was always strongly for intervention. I learned later that he had read *Mein Kampf* in 1940 and saw the coming debacle. On the other hand, Mom started out favoring neutrality in 1939, a position held by the WIL (and the majority of the population at that time, 80 percent). Later she realized that this was a battle we had to win, and she participated in the war effort.

Food
- Many Westonites grew Victory Gardens. Canning was a big deal. We were the only ones in town with a dehydrator. I remember the smell of the machine in action, and how Mom sealed and labeled each output in waxed paper. All the veggies except carrots tasted like cardboard.
- Mom would send us out to the woods to harvest fiddleheads and dandelions "because we are at war." We managed to eat them only if they were dressed with bacon and vinegar.
- Families contributed time and resources to start a hot lunch program at Hurlbutt School. Mom often delivered food and worked in the school kitchen—which buzzed during summers when all the mothers in town were urged to bring vegetables from their gardens to freeze and can. For five cents, pupils could get a meal of chicken, dumplings, a vegetable, and dessert. A government subsidy provided milk.

War Secrecy
- Occasionally Dad traveled to Hanford, Oregon. After the war, he told us the trips related to a GE contract connected to the development of the A bomb.
- We knew Willard Thorp, our friend and neighbor on Valley Forge, was doing something important for the war. He was a mysterious figure whom we rarely saw. His wife, Hildegard, was busy at home raising goats. Later we found he had worked closely with Franklin Roosevelt's New Deal programs, was Harry Truman's Assistant Secretary of State helping to draft the Marshall Plan, and, later, headed economic missions for John F. Kennedy and with the United Nations. After the war, he participated in the Paris Peace Talks.

Local War Efforts
- Gathering milkweed pods on Blueberry Hill for Air Force life jackets.

The Marching and Chowder Club
- Members (such as R. L. Duffus, Jimmy Daugherty, and Van Wyck Brooks) met at least once a month at members' houses. The host

selected a hike, and afterwards there were drinks, dinner prepared by the ladies (often in long skirts), and maybe charades. I remember several times when Duffus got a call from the *Times* and had to dictate an editorial about the war.

Scenes Around Town

- Dutee Hall rehearsing the neighborhood kids for Christmas sing-alongs.
- Wanting to strangle the Leopolds for letting their dogs free to roam, who nearly killed poor Bonnie, and how Louise kept Bonnie alive, changing dressings at all hours. I close my eyes and remember the acrid smell of the medicine.
- Outrageous Fred Davis, scaring the hell out of us little kids; how he loved to drive his old rattletrap car down Lyons Plains Sunday mornings, honking his horn.
- Going to the train station in the "puddle jumper," cooped up on the ledge in the back seat while Dad and Joe Leopold chatted away.

Living World War II: One Family in Weston, Connecticut, 1939-1945

Recollections
of the Weston War Years
Louise Hill
(now Lisa Paulson)

Connection to the Land
- I loved the wilderness quality in Weston, the great natural beauty of open, wild spaces at that time. The ability to ride off on my bicycle to sit on a rock at the edge of the reservoir and watch the sun setting over pristine hills, or to get lost in dense woods. Or to sit scribbling poems in solitary bliss on a gnarled root cantilevered over the swirling Saugatuck River at the bottom of our field . . .
- Skating up the frozen river (during the rare winters when it was cold enough to freeze) beneath dark, overhanging hemlock boughs, I felt like a mythic Nordic ice maiden.

Rites of Passage and Passions
- Miss Comer's ballroom dance classes in Westport when I was in the seventh grade represented a memorable introduction to the societal mores of growing up in that relatively "proper" era. I had to acquire full-length evening dresses—my favorite a heavy turquoise satin. The routine began with girls and boys lining up in pairs outside the ballroom (in the library building), each wearing spotless white gloves. We entered the big gym and marched two-by-two up to the receiving line in the center to shake hands with Miss Comer and a couple of hostesses (mothers). The boys bowed and the girls curtseyed. Then the girls all lined up along one wall with the boys opposite. At a signal, the boys rushed across the room to choose a partner for the first dance. Because there were always more girls than boys, the girls not picked

had to dance with each other. It was something of a painful popularity contest, where the "wallflowers" were literally left out, their discomfort on full display. Before the classes, often there were small regional dinner parties staged by the mothers; a few boys and girls were driven to various homes to eat and then ferried to the class. I went to a couple of these around Weston. One time my father arrived to pick me up after a class, and was in time to watch one hundred fifty kids grabbing each other's waists and snaking around in a conga line.

- From shy, wallflower status before age thirteen and for several years after, I suddenly in eighth grade miraculously caught the eye of several very green, equally shy young swains—one recently escaped from the Nazis in France, who exuded a mysterious Gallic charm and looks, the other an aspiring concert pianist with considerable savoir faire. I promptly developed serial crushes on these two. Now, seventy years later, whenever I smell lilacs, I'm immediately transported back to heady May evenings when I strolled hand-in-hand with Bill from France, past the fragrant bushes on Lyons Plains, both of us so painfully self-conscious that we were completely tongue-tied.

- At the other end of the dance spectrum were the frequent square dances held around Weston, either at the school or in the Emmanuel Church basement. Dutee Hall's band, with a caller, officiated at the latter. These were important (and sweaty) social events, not only because we got to show off our proficiency at swinging in perfect rhythm with our partners, but also because we could flirt and sample the best catches of the opposite sex (we came in packs of boys or girls, not with dates). Highlight of the evening was "Birdie in the Cage," where those in each square took turns dancing around one couple that was whirling dizzily in the center. When they ended with a daring kiss, everyone clapped. For this dance, it was important to get the right partner.

- Long before the age of cancer awareness, tanning was *de rigueur* for seventh and eighth graders. It was the fashion to go out with our girlfriends to lie endlessly under the blazing summer sun in two-piece bathing suits, happily burning to a crisp and then peeling. Tanned legs were a vanity issue, and when we couldn't get silk stockings during the war, we applied a liquid orange leg makeup. (Silk was needed for parachutes, and nylons were not yet on the scene.)

- In eighth grade, my mother bought me a new wool suit (at Macy's, for seven dollars). Up to this point, all of my clothes were either sewn by Mother or were hand-me-downs from relatives. This had dusty grey checks, and I remember the first time I wore it so proudly up to the school bus stop by the church, paired with new navy-and-white saddle shoes—a huge thrill. I can smell that wool even now.
- My first cigarette was smoked with a couple of other girls, egged on by thirteen-year-old Robie Harrington, behind Robie's barn by Cartbridge Road. It wasn't very satisfying, but we felt properly daring and "initiated." I was fourteen.
- Many adolescent girls develop a passion for horses. Mine, though, was goats. I recall promising the powers-that-be I'd stop any number of nasty habits if only my parents would let me raise goats. When they relented, partly because it was a patriotic thing to do in wartime—produce your own food—and also because they knew it would improve my sense of responsibility and self-reliance, I was in heaven.

There were tough times, especially on frigid, winter, pre-dawn mornings when I had to go to the barn in the dark to muck out the stall and milk Bonnie. Here was my typical routine:

It's 6:00 a.m. and a sharp wind is whipping away the last stars. The thermometer reads minus 15. In the light from the faint pallor to the East, I slip around crazily on rough ice, balancing my bucket of hot water. I can just make out the goat barn ahead. Once inside, in the comparative stillness, I pause to listen to the gentle creaking of the rafters. Scattered hayseeds are swirling on the floor, blown up by the wind from beneath wide cracks in the boards. Teetering on a plank high up that forms a crude hayloft, I toss down huge armfuls of musty clover and alfalfa, releasing clouds of choking dust.

Inside the goat stall, Bonnie and Bambi lie huddled together, shivering slightly. Bonnie complains of the unusually bitter cold with little questioning bleats, and lurches to her feet. She paws the platform impatiently. Bambi struggles up too, thrusts her head into the feed trough, and butts her empty pan in anticipation.

With Bonnie on the milking stand, I lean into her furry flank, ready to grab her leg in case she decides to stick it in the milk bucket. She's producing well, and I lug the warm pail into the kitchen, weigh the milk, strain it through cheesecloth, and record the amount. Next, carrying water and hay, I escort the goats down to the lower goat house where they'll spend the day. After forking out the dirty hay and sweeping the night stall, I must hustle to get ready for school.

In warm weather, I hike out to the dewy field and pound in stakes to tether the goats for the day. Frequently we have to chase them when they escape from their smaller fenced corral and get into the neighbors' gardens or, worse, nibble poisonous laurel or hellebore leaves.

For five years, I was a happy goatherd, running my own small business selling milk to my family and a couple of neighbors with special medical needs. I also served as midwife a number of times, and was round-the-clock nurse when Bonnie was mauled by the neighbors' dogs. Mostly I just loved my "goat people."

- I began cello lessons at age thirteen with our minister friend, Clyde Holbrook. At a certain point, he passed me on to Lief Rosanoff. Mr. Rosanoff had studied with Pablo Casals and also taught at the Julliard School of Music. Summers I went to his house in Wilton, and in colder weather, I took the train into New York. There I had to navigate the subways, hoisting my cello over my head at turnstiles, and then hanging onto it for dear life as the wind whistled through the steep concrete canyons and threatened to tear it away. My journey to the Rosanoffs' apartment took me past Columbia University where, during the war, I saw Navy midshipmen drilling in uniform past the main steps. I remember that once Mr. R. let me take my lesson on his Stradivarius cello and being amazed at how it almost seemed to play itself.

Around the Neighborhood

- Our near neighbors, the Dutee Hall family, soon became close friends, especially because Willy was in my class. There were endlessly fascinating activities to partake of in the eccentric Hall household (they lived in the parsonage next to the church). The four boisterous, creative Hall kids attracted a host of neighborhood youngsters, so the house was usually buzzing with projects. Here's a scene I might find on entering: in one room, full of kids, a newspaper is just going to press. In another, Willy (who later worked under architect Mies Van der Rohe) has designed and is building an intricate construction. Jerry Hall is glued to the radio fanatically cheering on his beloved Brooklyn Dodgers, or declaring ardent support for the plight of downtrodden factory workers (I believe he and his father, Dutee, might have been card-carrying members of the Communist Party, and Jerry eventually moved to California to work for labor union rights). Nancy and Clarissa have a nature project going and have been out collecting specimens, but they're willing to stop immediately if somebody brings out the cards to suggest gin rummy. Dutee, who plays a mean fiddle, is practicing for an upcoming square dance his band is playing for. And Leota, with professional wordsmith friend Phil Krapp, is vociferously arguing English poetry, pacing the living room, waving her cup of tea. She's ahead of her time as a proponent of herbal remedies and teas, often leading expeditions into the fields and woods to identify and gather wild plants. She may stop orating to shout "That dratted cat!" (Min-Cat was one of several prowling family felines who were forever getting into opened cans of tuna left around the kitchen.) There always seemed to be a faint fish aroma. This was one house where no one ever knocked but waded freely into the entertaining, chaotic fray.

- A winter ritual for several years involved Willy and Nancy coming to our house to sprawl on the floor in front of the fireplace, where my mother read to us the classics, such as *The Last of the Mohicans* and *The Three Musketeers*. She also started the three of us on Latin and French lessons.
- When gas rationing came on, Mother had to bite the bullet and get on a bicycle for the first time. I still have visions of her wobbling back and forth up Lyons Plains (always wearing a skirt or dress), determined to learn in order to serve as an air raid warden.
- I can still hear Franklin Roosevelt's stentorian proclamation booming out on our dining room Philco radio on December 7, 1941: "WE ARE AT WAR!"
- Often in winter, we skied or sledded on the long hill behind radio commentator Raymond Gram Swing's house. I remember when I was in eighth grade, Johnny Swing (in seventh) was sledding with us, along with a shy, curly-haired boy who was staying with his family; he was one of the hundreds of kids sent over from Britain to escape the London Blitz and the bombing throughout England.
- The only one in the family with the stomach to slaughter the chickens was Mother. This was supposed to be Doug's job, and he would spend inordinate amounts of time sharpening his axe and setting up the stump, delaying the moment of execution. If he couldn't bring himself to the task (neither my father nor I could stand to be in the vicinity), my mother would coolly step in, and soon a hapless, headless fowl was careening around the yard spraying blood. Then both Doug and I were expected to pitch in to pluck and then burn off the pinfeathers (that smell lingers still in my memory.)
- In summertime, there'd often be a call from Peggy Moore or Lillian Delarmy or Leota Hall, all from down Lyons Plains, saying the wild strawberries or blueberries were ripe—did we want to come along on a picking expedition? We'd drop everything, grab our buckets, and tramp up to the brambly fields off Eleven O'Clock Road or Kellogg Hill—anticipating a fine pie that night.

- Symphony conductor Fritz Reiner, who lived a half mile up Davis Hill Road, occasionally rode the commuter bus to go into New York. His chauffeur would drive him down to wait at the bus stop in front of our house. One time, hearing me practicing cello, he was curious. He came to the door and sat down to chat about my musical ambitions. I found him friendly and encouraging.
- Also on the subject of my cello and the commuter bus, one day I was riding the bus and noticed that Helen Keller and her companion, Polly, were also aboard. Gathering my courage, I fell into conversation with her through the companion. We got to talking about my cello playing. Miss Keller brightened, saying this was her favorite instrument. She perceived it "like wind in the pines."
- Mrs. Kearns, our dynamic, ninth-grade Latin teacher in Westport, was always thinking up creative ways to bring the "dead language" to life. When she suggested to our Latin club an authentic banquet, I invited the class out to our house. We "patricians" all came draped in togas (sheets) and reclined on the floor to dine (the menu written on scrolls in beautiful calligraphy—in Latin, of course). There happened to be a blizzard that night, and I remember that Tony Delano (class whiz) ended up walking all the way home to Saugatuck. [By 1943, we could no longer use cars for such frivolity.]
- It was a spring ritual for my father to organize the "burning of the fields," one of his favorite occupations, probably because it entailed a certain amount of danger and daring. He'd collect the small fry from the neighborhood and set a small fire barrier, and then all of us kids would stand around the periphery, beating the flames with shovels to make sure they were contained. Only once or twice did they get away and we had to summon the fire department. My mother—ordinarily fearless—had a phobia about fire and always retreated to the house during this operation. Some of the kids were nervous too, but we weren't given much choice.
- Living in the remote rural countryside, there were almost no extracurricular activities school kids could participate in (no way to

get home). So the closest I came to belonging to any group or sports team was joining the nearby pickup softball games. Summer evenings after dinner, all the neighbor children (of varying ages and talents) gathered to play at the vacant field next to the parsonage. By day, they congregated at our house to swim in the Saugatuck, swinging out on the rope tied to a big sycamore on the bank and then dropping into deep water. Jerry Hall's favorite stunt was walking along the river bottom, carrying heavy stones to see how long he could stay under.

- My mentor in my high school years was Adelaide Baker, a family friend in Westport who was active in peace circles and later served as a U.N. observer. It was she who persuaded me to apply for a Quaker work camp stint in summer 1944. The camp that accepted me was in Barnesville, Ohio, not far from the West Virginia border. This proved to be a fine and very unusual kind of experience. We were housed in the dormitory of a Quaker boarding school in the middle of the town. The dozen kids in our camp came from all around the country, mostly from cosmopolitan backgrounds, and I'm sure we startled or shocked the folks in this very conservative, isolated community. All the local women still wore long black skirts and poke bonnets, and the men were seen only in black suits and stovepipe hats. They addressed each other as "thee" (but not "thou"—which had fallen into disuse). Students might address a faculty member as "Teacher Charles Standing." "Mr." or "Mrs." would have been too formal.

We saw a posted list of regulations for the Quaker high schoolers. Girls were allowed two skirts and three sweaters of subdued colors—absolutely no reds or large plaids; checks could be no larger than three-quarters of an inch. All skirts had to be three inches below the knee when sitting. They wore dresses for limited athletics (slacks or shorts were considered indecent) and high cotton stockings in all weathers. Boys might be expelled for wearing a tie or bright socks—too frivolous for Quakers.

And here we were, brazenly sunning ourselves on the lawn in haltertops and shorts!

Students' families had to sign a statement saying they were harboring no musical instruments in their homes. Whistling and singing were not permitted inside school buildings. And, course, any sort of dancing was outlawed.

When we attended the Quaker meeting, all females sat on one side of the aisle, the males were on the other. Our work project was pruning, thinning, and picking in a large fruit orchard. From the tops of our ladders in the trees, we had a glorious time talking philosophy and politics with our leaders from Philadelphia. One was Martin, a charismatic young German (unusual and somewhat daring in the middle of this war, but something the Quakers would flaunt). Another was a delightful young woman, Becky Boone, a distant Kentucky cousin of Daniel.

- Dutee Hall played a major part in Christmas activities around Lyons Plains, working up unusual music. The neighbors often congregated at our house for holiday parties where everybody sang, Mother played piano, Dutee was on violin, Clyde Holbrook or I on cello, and Nancy and Clarissa on their recorders. Following the annual "gathering of the greens," our tree had been duly felled and dragged from the hemlock forest, along with fragrant boughs to decorate the front door and mantel.
- Another holiday ritual was the caroling procession that started at Emmanuel Church and ended a couple of miles up Valley Forge Road at the Harlans'. Here's what I remembered of one year and later wrote up:

A pale sliver of moon illuminated the little knot of us young people hunched darkly against the blue snow. We turned our collars up and marched along the lonely stretch of road. It was bitterly cold, a silent, relentless cold that snatched our breath away. Massive hemlocks loomed up on our left, bending under a foot of snow.

No one spoke. Scarves were muffled around our noses, heads bent in mute determination. I was getting awfully cold; my ears and nose ached and were fast turning numb. Soon the only way I knew I was still walking was by the snow squeaking under my boots. The eyes of the little nine-year-old beside me were desperate and frightened, but he trudged on bravely without a word. I kept telling myself this was the night everyone had looked forward to all year—the exhilaration of a night adventure, companionship, gaiety, music. What was it really, though, but an exquisite, endless torture?

Suddenly, I knew. A hoarse exclamation went up from our leader, and we saw a faint glow ahead. Mittens were pulled off, the cold forgotten. Matches were hurriedly scratched, lighting a host of candles. At the signal, "Here We Come Awassailing" broke out, growing stronger and richer as we approached the first house. At the last note, the door burst open and we poured in, taking in the burning logs spitting and popping in the fireplace, a great bowl of mulled punch, and a fiddler giving out snatches of carols. The spice of evergreens hung over the room, and everywhere were boisterous, laughing revelers. Had I really thought this wasn't the best night of the year? This was Christmas Eve in Weston.

End Notes

As terrible as the war years were, and despite the myriad inconveniences, the fact that they were tinged with the flavor of the often surreal, idyllic life we had built in that precise time span—1939 to 1945—made our sojourn in Weston an almost magical time in my memory. No doubt part of this was because everyone in town (and in the country) drew closer together, both because sharing was necessary, and because everyone was united behind the massive threats of a brutal war. A sense of community developed that was considerably stronger at that time than in our more politically fragmented life now.

My memories are rich with many subsequent visits to my parents' home after 1959, with my husband, two sons, and their families. Yet it was that earlier time in Weston, exactly bracketing the war years, that hold a special significance. That encapsulated period—that life—has, for me, ballooned to almost mythic proportions.

Of course, there were hardships. We scraped along with limited fuel, tires, shoes, stockings, meat, sugar, butter, and much more (often with unpleasant substitutes). We had to bike or walk when we could no longer drive our cars. Clearly there was terrible anxiety in families with servicemen, who died in great numbers. (Three out of four older brothers of a high school classmate were killed.) I was fortunate to be just under the age when my contemporaries might be drafted. But there was a sense that this was a just, "good" war. There was enthusiasm and strong patriotism when we entered the conflict in 1941. It was a time for heroism. For me, there was a romantic aura about the era:

all America was unified in a singular purpose. We put our military in their uniforms on a pedestal; they were going to save Europe, defeat Hitler, then Japan. There was a righteousness, even a fierce joy, about living with the sacrifices and hardships. We reveled in our Victory Gardens, in volunteering for defense work, supporting the troops, entertaining them, rolling bandages, darkening our windows with blankets, spotting planes.

The petty kinds of concerns—small crimes and misbehaviors—seemed to melt away or recede significantly in the face of our collective task.

Yes, these are memories to cherish.

About the Authors

W. Scott Hill came to live in Weston twice, in 1939 and in 1959. Born in Michigan in 1902 and raised in Reno, Nevada, he traveled east after college to work as an engineer for G.E. in Schenectady.

He met his wife Betty there in 1923 at an ice skating party where she was a social worker for the YWCA. They married in 1925.

Over the years, G.E. moved Scott to New York, Buffalo, Baltimore, Pittsfield, and back to Schenectady. A final stint was in New York again, allowing Scott and Betty to return to Weston in 1959 to land they had purchased there during World War II. They built a home in the community they cherished, where they lived for the rest of their lives.

Scott was active in the Aspetuck Land Trust, Weston Watershed Committee, Norfield Church projects, the Red Cross, The Community Council, and Y's Men of Westport/Weston. He served as president of the Weston Historical Society, where he helped to record oral histories of elders in the town. His work with G.E. evolved to recruitment of engineers, management, and contracts with the Navy during the War.

He died in 1995 at age 93. Betty followed in 2001 at 102.

Louise Hill (Lisa Paulson)

As Scott's daughter, and as a writer and artist, Lisa has spent a lifetime chasing and recording offbeat experiences. Whether traveling or living abroad with her professor husband Belden, she has been drawn to cultures at points of upheaval or profound change—as well as to spots worldwide of great natural beauty or unusual attraction. With Bel, in the 1970s, she founded the High Wind community, a rural enclave in eastern Wisconsin focused on ecology, education, and spirit.

Currently Lisa and Bel divide their time between the countrysides of Wisconsin and Vermont. Both of them have been inspired to reflect on and write about their family histories, adventures, and ideas.

Books by Lisa Paulson

*Living World War II: One Family in Weston, Connecticut
Memorable Letters and Experiences*
is available through Amazon

Of Stones and Spirits: Sixty Years of Travel
is also available through Amazon

*An Unconventional Journey: The Story of High Wind,
From Vision to Community to Eco-Neighborhood*

Voices From a Sacred Land: Images and Evocations
(the latter two available through Thistlefield Books)

www.ingramcontent.com/pod-product-compliance
Lightning Source LLC
Chambersburg PA
CBHW060204050426
42446CB00013B/2980